Married
to My
Garden

Barbara Blossom Ashmun

illustrations by Kaye Synoground

WILLIAM, JAMES & CO.

Wilsonville, Oregon

Publisher	Jim Leisy
Production Editor	Tom Sumner
Publicity	Kat Ricker
Cover Arrangement	Charlotte Klee
Cover Photo	Jim Leisy

Printed in China

Rights and Permissions
William, James & Co.
8536 SW St. Helens Drive, Ste. D
Wilsonville, Oregon 97070

Library of Congress Cataloging-in Publication Data

Ashmun, Barbara.
    Married to my garden / Barbara Blossom Ashmun ; illustrated by Kaye Synoground.
        p. cm.
    ISBN 978-1-59028-193-2
    1. Gardening. I. Title.
    SB455.3.A84 2007
    635.9092--dc22
                                2006102003

Contents

Contents

Acknowledgments

I think, in the long run, that to find people who support

your work, it's best not even to think in literary terms

but to look for easygoing and open-hearted human

beings with a low threshold of embarrassment, who,

generally speaking, aren't beset by terror,

fear, or . . . "scarcity consciousness."

—Carolyn See

WITHOUT MY PARTNER Tom Robinson, *Married to My Garden* would not have been published in this form. He envisioned a bound book with illustrations and a beautiful cover instead of the modest chapbook I had in mind ("Your work deserves better," he urged). Tom bought us both laptops and proceeded to format the book for publication as quickly as I polished the text, managing the differences between the PC and Mac worlds with patience and humor. Tom is not a gardener, so when he read the manuscript and laughed and cried, any last doubts I had all but vanished.

Thanks to my writing group buddies, Jebra Turner, Nancy Woods, Trudy Hussman and Cindy McKitrick for helping me decide which essays to include and for encouraging me to go forward with publication. Extra thanks to Trudy Hussman for proofreading and to Jebra Turner for being my promotion and marketing mentor. Special appreciation to Marian Kuch for proofreading the final draft.

I write in solitude without the readymade network of a workplace, so I am especially appreciative of loving friends who listen with the "third ear" and are there for me as much in good times as in tough times—Pauline Anderson-Smith, my sister Sarita Eisenstark, Mary Huey, La Verne Kludsikofsky, Charlotte Klee, Marian Kuch, Janet Lewis, Anita Morrison, Connie O'Reilly, Megs Patton, Virginia Plainfield, Jebra Turner, and Martha Wagner.

What a thrill to witness magic, as artist Kaye Synoground transformed my words into the evocative images that illustrate this book. I am grateful for the imagination, skill, patience and perseverance that she brought to the "look" of the book.

Kudos to Charlotte Klee for the beautiful bouquet on the cover. When I asked her to help me select flowers and arrange them, I trusted that her eye for beauty and imagination would be just what we needed, but in fact the results surpassed my dreams.

My thanks to Robert Beatty and the Portland Insight Meditation Community for invaluable spiritual guidance and support.

Many of these essays were inspired by visits to private gardens and nurseries, in numbers too great to list. My deep appreciation to all the generous gardeners who shared their time and knowledge with me over the years.

Thanks also to the publications that were early homes to some of these reflections, especially *The Woman's Journal* and Hardy Plant Society of Oregon's *Bulletin*.

For my Remarkable Tom,
With Enduring Love

Introduction

A little garden in which to walk, and immensity in which

to dream. At one's feet that which can be cultivated and

plucked; overhead that which one can study and meditate

on: some herbs on earth, and all the stars in the sky.

—Victor Hugo

FOR MANY YEARS I've been intrigued by why we garden and what becomes of us when we're smitten with the love of plants. For me, gardening began innocently enough. Soon after I moved to Portland, Oregon from New York City in 1972, I bought a home that came with a yard. Suddenly there were roses to prune so that the mailman could navigate to the letter slot without getting stabbed, and huge hulking rhododendrons to dig up and give away so that sunlight would once more shine through the living room windows.

Before long I was feasting on homegrown tomatoes and cucumbers thanks to my next door neighbor Frank, who brought me seeds and showed me how to sow them. I thought I'd moved to Portland to earn my M.S.W. and become a better social worker, but life had other plans for me. The garden seduced me, and what started out as a flirtation became a lifelong passion.

Some friends worried about my sanity, and voiced concern about my obsession with plants. "If you're always gardening, how will there ever be room for a man in your life?" they asked, trying to shake me back to reality. After all, I was divorced, and not getting any younger. Not that I didn't date—it was just that often the garden was more compelling, and my efforts there were so much more fruitful. In fact love for gardening made me a writer, brought me wonderful new friends, and gave me purpose. And eventually, the best man in the world showed up at an event directly related to the garden. Tom fell for me when he heard me speaking at a book signing for my fifth book, *Garden Retreats: Creating an Outdoor Sanctuary*, which just goes to show you that if you follow your heart, love will find you even in the midst of work.

For many years learning the plants and their botanical names, how they grew and how to plant them artistically, took all my attention. Then as I became more immersed, and the garden changed me into a more patient, attentive, reflective person, I became more interested in why we fall in love with gardening and how that connection transforms us.

I wrote these short essays over a period of two decades, as the spirit moved me. Earlier versions of some pieces were published in The Hardy Plant Society of Oregon's *Bulletin*, *The Gardener's Almanac* and *The Woman's Journal*. But many more essays remained in the files, waiting for a home.

Then early in 2001 I got a phone call from my friend, writer Nancy Woods, who had organized The Funny Ladies, a group of women who write for a living, and also for fun. She invited me to read with them at Broadway Books, an independent bookstore here in Portland. I read "Just a Fool in Love" and "Removing the Rose-Colored Glasses" to an audience of readers who were not necessarily gardeners, and they loved it. What a revelation—even nongardeners wanted to hear stories about the adventures and misadventures of a besotted gardener. But it shouldn't have come as such as a surprise. Gardening surely is one of life's most absurdly addictive undertakings, and we can all relate to the hopelessly obsessive folly of it all. Turning a slice of wilderness into a garden while Mother Nature is laughing her head off, sprinkling weed seeds, commandeering moles and launching hurricanes is not that different from sustaining a romance after five years of marriage.

I had such a good time with the Funny Ladies—reading with them reminded me of the pleasure I'd taken in writing in the early days, before I became a nationally known author, before deadlines, marketing, and promotion of book after book turned creativity into such serious work. I became nostalgic for lighter-hearted times when I'd written a column called "Samurai Gardener" just for fun, when I'd wake up with a poem in my heart, or tiptoe out to the dewy garden in my slippers to see if the poppies had opened yet.

Early in 2002 Funny Ladies went to press with *Assorted Nuts and Chews: Short Writings to Feed the Funny Bone.* Our little chap books with the sparkling red covers sold like hotcakes—people would flip through a copy, laugh, buy one for themselves and another for a gift.

Soon the seed for *Married to My Garden* sprouted. I would follow in the footsteps of Funny Ladies and publish my own collection of essays, just for fun. It wouldn't have to become a blockbuster, or go through the hoops of a publishing house—it would simply be a way to give my short pieces a home, to gather them together under one roof for readers to enjoy. It would be like planting all those perennials growing in containers on the patio in the garden beds at long last, and allowing them to settle into a more spacious landscape.

In many ways my life as a gardener followed the stages of romance. At first I was obsessed, and could think of little else. I would fall asleep at night dreaming of plants and wake up daydreaming about how I would arrange them, turning over color combinations in my mind. Like a woman in love, I was possessed, and most everything else seemed trivial. Friends who didn't garden dropped away, bored stiff, and new friends, similarly crazed, came along and became part of my life.

There came a point when too much of a good thing led to disenchantment—sore wrists, lower back pain and a losing battle with weeds and moles made me wonder about the whole affair. Yet all it took was a road trip or a vacation overseas to bring me to my senses. I couldn't live without the garden, even with all its faults. I was married to my garden for better or worse, but now in a more conscious way. It would never be perfect, but it's as good as it gets, a wonderful place to commune with plants, experience the wonder of life unfolding, and get to understand myself better.

If you're a gardener, I hope that these pieces will entertain and console you. You've already chosen a path that's endlessly intriguing—the garden opens the door to horticulture, agriculture, cooking, art, philosophy, spirituality, writing, carpentry, stonemasonry, sculpture, alchemy, you name it. If you haven't yet gardened, I hope that these essays will lure you into the back yard, and inspire you to get your hands dirty. May you allow the garden to cast its magic mantle upon you and bless you with all of its delicious fullness.

Obsession

Possessed

Let no one think that real gardening is a bucolic and meditative occupation. It is an insatiable passion, like everything else to which a man gives his heart.

—*Karel Capek*

WHEN I WAS FORTY-SOMETHING and had just moved to two-thirds of an acre, I was also dating Edward, who was determined to get married. One day we were out in the back yard, admiring the beginnings of flower borders, when he said with chagrin, "You'll never marry me, you're already married to your garden!"

At the time I laughed, and shrugged it off as the kind of remark that a disappointed suitor makes when he realizes he's not being taken seriously. Still, years later, his comment echoes in my mind, and I have to admit that to some degree he was right. In many ways I am married to my garden, and the bond only gets stronger each year.

I spend more time with my garden than with any friend. I even bought a miner's lamp to strap across my forehead so that I could garden at night. It's especially useful in winter when darkness falls at 4:30, and always handy for evening slug hunting—just when the slimy little things think it's safe to come out and graze on hosta leaves, I slip on surgical gloves and plop them into a coffee can filled with salty water.

Like a good wife, I protect the garden from an army of pests. I squash earwigs and snails, slice through cutworms, pinch leaf rollers, and wash away aphids. I tromp mole hills flat, chase away stray dogs and raccoons. I scan the borders for cress and thistle, dock and morning glory. Strapped to my belt is a holster housing a narrow trowel that will lift the deepest-rooting dandelion, the most stubborn buttercup.

I feed the garden regularly, and fortunately this requires little imagination, few shopping expeditions, no kitchen duty or culinary skills. The simplest of diets satisfies it—horse manure, chicken manure, rabbit litter, mushroom compost. I'm not tied to a schedule of mealtimes—any time will do. As for fresh ingredients, *au contraire*, the older and riper the better.

When it comes to communication, the garden is a flawless companion. I can say anything and it takes no offense. I might ruminate about some work project that went amuck, or a friend that disappointed, yet never a grumble from the garden, just the quiet rustle of grasses and the song of birds. "Ah now, this too will pass," I can almost hear the lilies whisper. A little waft of their fragrance and I feel calmer already.

If anger should get the best of me, half an hour of digging will cure it, and does the garden resent my taking it out on the soil? Not a bit—if anything it seems to heave a grateful sigh, aerated and ready to drain better. I can almost hear it murmur "Thanks for turning me over."

Most days my work is a complete pleasure, and I feel fortunate to have a garden filled with fragrant butterfly bushes, sweet figs and juicy pears. But occasionally I feel like a slave to the goddess Flora, and wonder if I made a terrible mistake investing in such a big place. Whatever was I thinking—that I would stay young forever?

Yet I remain loyal, tending my garden in all weather, envisioning how it will come to life again each spring as it has for 14 years past. I have flirted with other loves, but in the end it's the garden I return to with great attention and interest. The seeds for my books dwell in the garden; metaphors for poetry arise from its fertile soil. The garden is simply at the heart of everything I do and love.

Enslaved

He who cultivates a garden, and brings to perfection

flowers and fruits cultivates and advances

at the same time his own nature.

—*Ezra Weston*

THERE MUST BE AN EASIER HOBBY than gardening. One that doesn't ask you to slog across squishy lawns and muddy paths to look for the first slug-nibbled daffodils. One that doesn't require you to plant newly divided lilacs from a friend's garden in the pouring rain, which has suddenly turned to stinging hail accompanied by booming thunder.

It takes a certain kind of madness to tend a garden. Devoted gardeners pull their coats on over their nighties on freezing winter nights and rush out to cover a beloved daphne with a quilt. On hot summer days they start weeding in the damp dawn and keep going as the sun beats down, ignoring a heat headache at noon to water all the pots for the second time that day. They rise at 5 a.m. in order to wander through the borders before going to work, looking for the first open poppy, the first unfurled iris. They even drive out to a spring plant sale at daybreak on a Saturday morning, and stand in line for hours like some rock band groupie.

If all this weren't evidence enough of obsession, get this. Gardeners actually buy dirt. Yes, they spend money on manure, compost, sewage sludge, and topsoil, and would be ecstatic to be given a gift of any of these materials. Imagine—they'd happily take good money that could buy a bottle of French perfume and spend it on stinky soil amendments. Some of us even recycle our neighbors' garbage to make better soil, much to their disbelief.

My friend Mary still can't comprehend why I welcome her with a big smile whenever she brings me giant plastic bags bursting with spent straw and manure that she cleans out of her pet rabbits' hutches. "Are you sure you still want more?" she asks cautiously before she makes another delivery. My answer is always a loud "Yes!" With nearly an acre to tend, I never have enough compost for the beds and borders.

Right now I'm staring at a 20-foot-long bed piled three feet high with rabbit litter that's quietly decomposing. The worms are slithering through it, feasting and breaking it down, and a few robins are hopping across the top, pouncing on the worms and pulling them up like spaghetti. In a few months this bed will turn into lovely black soil, and I'll plant roses and perennials in the crumbly dirt. If there's one thing that's constant in the garden, it's change.

That's probably what keeps us fools slaving so hard, despite foul weather, voracious bugs and sore muscles. It's the one place in the world where we're sure to make a difference, where we're able to catalyze and witness change. Where prickly blackberries once sprawled, fragrant butterfly bushes bloom; where dock and dandelions bloomed, shrub roses and cranesbills flower. I can't improve the economy, but I can transform soil. I can't change the weather, but I can alter my mood. A whiff of 'Somerset' daphne or mock orange makes my spirits soar, even on the grayest day.

The garden changes us as much as we change it. Watching its nature, we are bound to learn by example. It shows us abundance—seedlings blanket the spring floor, whether cress or cosmos. It's a living example of patience. Trees stand quietly through the seasons, waiting it out through winter's cold and ice, bending their branches in the wind, and leafing out when spring's sun warms their branches. Peonies push up through the wet earth every spring, pulsing to the beat of a new season.

Best of all the garden turns us into florists. Right now on a March afternoon, a big bouquet brimming over with forsythia, flowering plum, camellia, flowering quince, daffodils and Lenten roses makes a splash of pink and yellow on my dining room table, thanks to my neighbor, Gavin Younie, who made it for me, and to all the other neighbors, who contributed branches whether they wanted to or not. Gardening may be hard work, but it gives as good as it takes.

Just a Fool in Love

Earth's crammed with Heaven.

—Elizabeth Barrett Browning

YOU CAN JUMP INTO GARDENING at any age, and without a lot of fuss. All you need is a patch of earth, a packet of seeds, and some water. A flower garden can be as natural as a wildflower meadow or as sophisticated as Sissinghurst—you decide.

You don't have to take classes or buy expensive tools, although it doesn't hurt to do either, if you like. You can dabble, putter, or pour your heart into gardening. You probably won't even know where that first step will take you until many years later.

If you're lucky, gardening will be like falling in love— you will lose all caution and become a fool in the best sense of the word. Webster's sixth definition is the one I like best: A fool is "a person with a talent or enthusiasm for a certain activity." When it comes to gardening, either talent or enthusiasm can carry you forward. If you have both, watch out! You'll be carried away, even swept away into a new life, one in which plants will occupy increasingly larger spaces in your imagination.

For example, when your partner looks deeply into your eyes early in the morning and asks what's on your mind, it may be hard to admit that you've been considering whether to take out all the grass in the parking strip to make a new perennial border, and that you've been turning over the idea of a hot versus cool color scheme. When you're standing out in the middle of the lawn staring, and your neighbor stops by to shoot the breeze, it will be all you can do to smile and be polite,

11

when you were right in the middle of visualizing the perfect combination of perennials to plant under the Japanese snowbell tree.

It will be almost impossible to jump up and greet your best friend when she comes upon you crouched between two stickery rose bushes, stretching as far as you can to dig out a thistle growing just beyond your reach. When you've pulled so hard on a stubborn root that you fall over backwards, you'll be thankful that you were in the furthest corner of the back yard, nowhere near the neighbor's deck.

Becoming a gardener calls for a very relaxed dress code. You'll wear baggy pants for crawling around in the dirt, waterproof boots for digging and slug stomping, layers of shirts, sweatshirts and vests to peel off as the day warms up, surgical gloves to keep your hands dry, and a fisherman's vest with dozens of pockets for labels, marking pens, seeds and Kleenex. Your hair will be mashed down under a sensible sunhat, or strewn with leaves, petals and seeds before the day is done. Forget about looking like Martha Stewart.

The best part of all is that you can be really stupid in the garden. No need for witty repartee when you're mindlessly turning the soil over and chopping it into crumbly bits with the edge of a spade. You can quietly concentrate on tracing the route of a buttercup through a bed of look-alike perennials, then dig it out with gusto. You can stare vacantly at an empty space in the garden and imagine how it will look filled with roses and lavender. Or cannas and sunflowers . . . or maybe a rock garden would be better.

You will be deeply upset by events that most adults would laugh about. A slug has bitten off a lily bud and you feel deep outrage. When moles lift your newly planted dahlias out of the ground your mind will boil with murderous thoughts—you may even rush out and set a trap. When rabbits graze on your prize clematis, leaving a big hole where the roots once were, you will remember with keen interest a friend's offer to "take care of them."

You will foolishly believe that soon the garden will be completed, that by next year you will have finished that last bed, that the design will be done and you will lie back in a hammock with an iced tea and enjoy the results. Little do you know that your taste has already been gradually changing, that you will soon no longer be pleased by pastels, that as a matter of fact they will bore you stiff. Orange and red will call to you and the idea of a fiery garden will become irresistible. Not only that, but you begin to see that the shapes of the existing beds are terrible and need to be altered, completely. That the natural pond that you dug three years ago in hopes of attracting herons has drawn weeds instead and was a really bad idea, and maybe needs to be filled in, right away.

When you began making a garden, perhaps it was all open and sunny, and you planted trees for shade. Five years later you have the shade you wanted, but oddly enough, the sun loving perennials aren't doing so well anymore. Or perhaps a wind storm has blown down the one big tree that cast shade on all the hydrangeas and astilbes, and now they're shriveling up in the sun, begging to be moved.

If there's one thing you can count on in the garden, it's change. The garden will change, and so will you. Don't even try to resist, just let the surprises sweep you along in their wake. After all, if it all stayed put, what would you do with all your time, your energy, your love?

Driven to Distraction

There's a part of the sun in the apple,

A part of the moon in a rose;

There's a part of the flaming Pleiades

In every leaf that grows.

—Augustus Wright Bamberger

EARLY ONE MORNING in July I went out to the garden for a few minutes to snip some purple moor grass foliage, the better to write about it for *Fine Gardening* magazine. Knowing it would be hard to resist the temptation to pull a few weeds or deadhead a daylily or two, I purposely didn't change into gardening grubbies, just pulled on my leather belt, through which my two trusty holsters are threaded—one holds a narrow-nosed trowel, the other Felco pruners. I marched toward the back border, but couldn't help noticing out of the corner of my eye that a half dozen new angelica seedlings had sprouted just where I thought I'd removed them all a week before. "Let me just dig out those few troublemakers before they root themselves down to China," I muttered to myself. A few stabs with the trowel and up sprung the carrot-like tap roots.

Looking up from the ground I noticed the delicate pale blue bells of 'Betty Corning' clematis shimmer as sunlight poured through them. In front of Betty globes of garlic flowers stood above sturdy stems, their papery skullcaps half off and half on, so I tugged one off and watched the newly released clusters of silky pink buds tremble.

Determined to get to the moor grass, I continued south, but along the chip path, wouldn't you know it, blue dune grass (*Elymus glaucus*) was once again running and rooting, so I dug out a few rompers heading for the next bed, just in the nick of time. That's when I saw the mulberries glistening in the sunlight like garnets. Stopping for a taste, I spotted a branch shaking violently—a squirrel was reaching repeatedly for fruit with its paws. We stood together there in the shade and feasted on the juicy berries, both of us happily occupied as time stood still. Worries about morning glory creeping under the fence and blackberry canes reaching over the fence completely disappeared. All that remained was sweetness bursting on the tongue, the song of birds, the gentle breeze, voices of neighbor children floating on the summer air, fingers turning purple.

Planted from a small whip some ten years ago, the mulberry tree grew almost unnoticed for several years, until burgundy fruit covered its branches and birds from all around gathered to peck and sing. If you haven't tasted a mulberry, call me up next July and come over—there's more than enough for birds, squirrels and friends.

I did eventually arrive where the variegated purple moor grass was gleaming in the morning sun, its slender leaves striped with creamy yellow. To my horror, a crop of *Verbena bonariensis* had seeded itself amid the grass and was poking up just high enough to be seen. It would take only a few minutes to pluck out the seedlings by hand at this early stage, before they rooted down and would need a spade to remove them. That's when I noticed that 'Chocolate Chip' bugleweed (*Ajuga*) was also creeping through the nearby Lenten roses (*Helleborus orientalis*) and if I didn't stop the runners right this minute, it would be too late. No more than ten minutes, I bargained with myself. I'd come back later with the spade and dig out the bugleweed crowns.

It really was time to get back to the house to write.

But on the way back the velvet flowers of wine-colored 'Niobe' clematis caught my eye, and I stopped to pick one. The six petals were separated by enough space to let each stand out, and all together they made a perfect pinwheel of a flower. The central stamens were palest yellow against the dark velvet burgundy. Nearby Spanish love-in-a-mist (*Nigella hispanica*) was turning an island bed into a meadow, blue flowers hovering above the ferny foliage and dark central eyes already forming spidery black seedpods. I stopped to deadhead a few maroon daylilies, and their dark purple juice stained my hands, mingling with the dye of the wine-colored mulberries.

I was making very slow progress in the direction of the house and beginning to wonder if going inside was even possible. 'Honorine de Brabant,' a Bourbon rose with pink stripes, beckoned. I stopped for a whiff of sweet perfume and saw that 'Etoile Violette' clematis had exploded and was almost smothering the rose—together they looked like a purple blanket with small pink patches where the roses were struggling through. I picked one of each to take inside, gathered one last handful of mulberries for the road, and with a deep sigh said good-bye to the garden, at least for a while.

Addicted to Flowers

The lesson I have thoroughly learnt, and wish

to pass on to others, is to know the enduring

happiness that the love of a garden gives.

—Gertrude Jekyll

MY FIRST ADVENTURES in the garden were with vegetables, and there's a certain suggestive photograph of me from the '70s. I'm wearing a long flowery dress, proudly pointing to a foot-long English cucumber that's growing up a trellis on the side of the garage.

But after a dazzling visit to Butchart Gardens I began growing flowers, and vegetables took a back seat. Flowers captured my attention in a more compelling way. Oriental poppies with furry leaves suddenly sprouted stout stems with promising buds at the tips. One June morning the fuzzy sepals popped open and dropped to the ground, and huge, red, crepe-papery petals unfurled. A mysterious black center punctuated the poppy's red heart, with a garnish of silky stamens. I stared and stared, forgetting my terrible job as a medical social worker, forgetting my faltering marriage.

Some mornings I couldn't wait for the poppies to open, and I'd pry the buds apart with my fingernails so I could drink in a fresh flower at the start of the day. That made going to work much more tolerable. Some days, when the smells and sounds of the hospital were unbearable, I'd drive home on my lunch hour and sniff the cottage pinks. Clove-scented, they restored my spirit. I'd rub lavender and rosemary leaves and feel soothed. The healing power of fragrance helped me face the difficult job of counseling the sick and the dying.

17

At first it was the beauty of individual flowers that captured my attention—the complexity of purple bearded irises with upper petals rising up like the arms of a ballerina, and lower petals flouncing down like a tutu. Velvety ruffles that deserve a better name than beards peeked out from between the two tiers.

Electrifying colors woke me up—magenta cranesbills, cobalt blue gentians and fire-engine-red poppies. An array of roses thrilled me, from pastel pink to nearly black, with flowers as simple as apple blossoms, as elaborate as the quartered white 'Madame Hardy' with a green button eye at the center. Their scents were delicate as face powder, delicious as vanilla, and evocative as myrrh.

Then the artist in me, that had been dormant since junior-high-school art classes, woke up too. I became aware of the bigger picture and wanted to paint with flowers as my palette. How could I mediate between orange poppies and pink peonies that bloomed together, clashing horribly? Would a touch of blue delphinium or a drift of gray artemesia make the difference? The pleasure I experienced in the garden now took a quantum leap. I not only tended individual plants but orchestrated them.

Engrossed in this complex endeavor, working with color and texture, simultaneous and sequential bloom, my concentration was intense. The world could come to an end and I'd still be staring ahead intently, picturing the outcome next year when 'Westerland' rose, now nothing but a bundle of sticks, would form a cloud of coral, with a pool of lavender catmint at its feet. Hours would disappear as I weeded around existing plants, daydreaming about next summer's color schemes.

For the first time in my life, solitude became a pleasure. In the quiet company of flowers, my own thoughts and feelings unfolded too. While my fingers were busy deadheading daylilies, my mind was free to ramble and roam, sifting through the debris of the day, sorting, making sense of what mattered and discarding the junk. Before long, all my internal noise quieted down, and my mind became as calm as the flowers. I relaxed, free to just be with colors, with fragrances, with dreams. With an iridescent beetle, lumbering along at the base of a pile of leaves, or a slippery earthworm, probing its way into the damp earth.

As the years passed and I became familiar with the seasonal cycles, the joy of growing flowers increased. Perennials return year after year, pushing up from the wet soil in late winter, unfolding their leaves, forming buds, flowering and setting seed in a comforting, predictable rhythm. No matter how chaotic my life might be, no matter how many anticipated and unanticipated changes occurred, I could count on my flowers to come back.

Mostly, they returned bigger and better. The garden gives back far more than I ever give it. Abundance is the rule—roots and rhizomes creep steadily outward, seedpods explode, shooting surprises where I least expect them—in distant beds and borders, even in the crevices of sidewalks and stairways. Blue peach-leaved bellflowers, forget-me-not, love-in-a-mist and yellow lady's mantle have traveled the full span of my garden. Who says plants can't walk?

Sometimes there are losses. A ten-year-old daphne dies for no good reason, a sumptuous rose bush succumbs to rust, and all the penstemons drown in a flood. At first I'm devastated by the damage. And then, with time, inspiration comes for renewal. Now there's space to try out some of the newest English roses or a hibiscus that's been patiently waiting in its pot on the patio. Growing flowers is about death, but also about new life. There's always hope that next year's borders will be even better— more colorful, more fragrant, and that the flowers will come together in sweeter harmony.

They say that gardeners live longer, and attribute it

to the benefits of fresh air and exercise. But the truth is that we simply can't wait for the next spring when once again we turn our attention to growing flowers, watching with great attention for the return of our familiar friends as they emerge from their winter rest. Old gardeners remember past seasons but live on for next summer when there will be yet another chance to play in the dirt.

Seduced by Sunflowers

. . . then a craze for specialization breaks out in
him, which makes of a hitherto normal human being
a rose, dahlia, or some other kind of exalted maniac.

—Karel Capek

FIRST YOU VISIT GARDENS all over the world and notice that you're stretching your neck a lot to look up. You feel exalted by plants that tower—bright yellow sunflowers, lavender Joe Pye weed, purple iron weed, and giant reed grass that reminds you of gargantuan corn. You start to understand that gardens, like cathedrals, benefit from height. You enjoy being dwarfed by big, skyscraping plants. You realize that tall plants make a garden look sensational.

Then you see sunflowers that have not just yellow petals, but mahogany, red, and orange rays, the kind Van Gogh would have painted. You admire their brazen hues and long to grow them in your own garden. You're embarrassed to discover how timid your color choices have been until now, restricted to safe blue and bashful pink, cowardly cream and conventional white. You decide to be more daring, to risk bold and even clashing colors, to plunge into the cauldron of persimmon orange and tomato red and mustard yellow. Next summer you will grow flowers that sizzle and smoke, that shock the neighbors silly.

When you get home from your travels you send for catalogs and browse through them, hunting for hot, brilliant colors. You find sunflowers with enticing names—Red Sun and Orange Sun, Sunburst Mixed and Velvet Queen. You order seeds by mail—Teddy Bear and

21

Music Box, Luna and Taiyo, Color Fashion Mixed and Mammoth Russian. You're fearless, abandoning all good sense in favor of recklessness. When it comes to colors, when it comes to your budget, you've gone over the top.

At winter garden shows you find still more varieties with irresistible names—Piccolo and Lion's Mane, Ring of Fire and Infrared. You decide that you're no longer interested in perennials or roses, that your mission this year is to display the world's largest collection of sunflowers.

Soon spring arrives and you're surrounded by seed packets, wondering what on earth possessed you to buy so many. How will you germinate them when you're scrambling to keep up with the weeding and pruning and mulching? When will you find the time to fuss with tiny seeds and sterile soil, and anyhow, what makes you think any of those seeds will sprout? What if they're all duds? Maybe you should just stash all those packets in the refrigerator and tackle them next year.

But one evening in March, a sense of urgency makes you grab the seed packets, a marking pencil and a large plastic bag of Dixie cups. Panic propels you down to the basement where your stash of plastic sweater boxes and fungicide and potting soil have been patiently waiting since last year's seed-starting frenzy.

Like gliding through an old familiar dance, you turn the Dixie cups upside down and punch drainage holes in their bottoms with an ancient shish-kebab skewer. You fill them with potting soil and set them neck to neck in the plastic boxes, gently so you don't tip them over, until you've filled all three containers. You water them from below with gallons of tepid water into which you've sprinkled a little fungicide to prevent the seedlings from damping off. As the Dixie cups soak up the water, you scribble Red Sun and Italian White and Teddy Bear on white plastic tags, so that some summer day when your sunflowers bloom, you will know which is which.

Then you open each packet and remove the big black seeds, dropping them one by one onto the surface of the soil in the Dixie cups, sticking an appropriate tag into each cup. You cover each seed with the smallest amount of dirt and snap the lids down on the plastic boxes. Last of all, you seal the packets of leftover seeds with tape and store them in the fridge for next year.

Each day you go down to the basement and peek into the boxes. At first the seedlings break through the soil's crust like cobra heads. Next they expand into pairs of small green leaves. Each day they very slowly rise higher on slender necks until they're pressed against the tops of the boxes. That's when it's time to remove the lids and set the boxes under fluorescent lights. You set the timers for sixteen hours of bright white light. You tap fertilizer crystals into gallons of room-temperature water, cap them, shake them upside down, and watch the water turn turquoise. You pour a half inch or so of this solution into each box of sunflower starts and wait.

Each day, you visit the seedlings and marvel. They begin growing in earnest, reaching for the lights. You raise the fixtures on their chains and s-hooks so that the lights are always about six inches above the new shoots. You worry. The sunflowers will get too leggy before May 15, your target planting date, or they will not grow quickly enough, or they will damp off and collapse, or the Dixie cups will disintegrate from all the moisture and fertilizer. You wonder if you should have used plastic pots, but no, it's too traumatic to knock young sunflowers out of plastic, and so much easier on the seedlings to cut away the paper. Like gardeners all over the world in the spring, you mumble to yourself a lot, fretting and fussing over your tender infant plants.

On May 13 you take the boxes of sunflower seedlings outside to harden off. This is their first exposure to wind and sun and rain, so you set them close to the house where they will be somewhat sheltered, and put Sluggo around the boxes to keep away the first likely predators. You prepare planting holes, adding compost and old chicken manure, remembering last year's fiasco when you planted your seedlings in packed clay and they languished. You make sure each sunflower has a foot and a half of space in full sun, having learned from experience that crowding and shade make them sulk.

On May 15 you take the boxes to the flower border, cut away the Dixie cups and carefully settle the new sunflowers into their planting holes. For good measure you put small twigs cut from apple branches around each plant so that neither your big foot nor the cats' small paws will trample the seedlings. You sprinkle a little Sluggo around each plant for good measure. Since it's nice and drizzly you don't have to water your new seedlings, but you will keep a careful eye on the weather and water with a rain wand should the rain cease. You will not leave home this spring, for you are now a responsible sunflower grower, and you must stick around all summer and fall to fertilize and deadhead. Nor would you want to travel this year, for the thrill of opulent mahogany, scarlet and vivid yellow sunflowers will surpass the most exotic foreign destination.

Getting in the Mood

Jumping In

We work in an exhilarating alliance with nature,

which is at once our muse and our nemesis,

our inspiration and our undoing.

—*Des Kennedy*

YOU CAN DIVE INTO GARDENING any time—the river has been there since Eden. I jumped in one June day in 1973, completely ignorant and full of curiosity. The soil in my yard was hard as a rock and gray as pewter. I tried digging ineffectively with my one-and-only crude shovel, and pretty soon I heard the thwack of my next-door neighbor Frank's screen door and the sound of his boots tromping across the lawn. I can still see his white hair, ruddy face and blue eyes twinkling behind his glasses.

Pretty soon he was at my side, hauling all the right tools for the job I was struggling with. He showed me how to swing a mattock like a pickax and chop into the baked clay, how to turn the soil over with a freshly sharpened spade and slice it into slivers like slices of bread, how to rake it smooth into fine crumbs. Frank loved to demonstrate, and it was all I could do to wrest the tools out of his thick farmer's hands and do the job myself.

Frank's basement was a cross between a hardware store and a garden center, full of freshly sharpened tools, wire, twine, lumber, fertilizer, bolts and nuts. Each rake and spade was hung on its proper hook. Screws and nails were housed by size in an immaculate array of baby food jars. The floor was covered with green linoleum and there were several retired old armchairs for us to sit in while he showed me how to start cucumber seeds in sphagnum moss or separate dahlia starts from last year's huge spidery clump with a sharp knife.

Frank taught me how to add gypsum, peat moss, chicken manure and compost to my heavy clay soil. At first everything I added was store-bought, but soon I followed his example and made a simple compost pile in the corner of the back yard. Frank's was just a big pile of vegetable peelings, grass clippings and leaves that he would turn occasionally until it became good dirt. I could always tell that the Curtis family had eaten cantaloupe for dinner or grapefruit for breakfast by the state of the compost pile.

In my small city garden there was a manageable amount of debris. I turned it once a week with a pitchfork and shoveled it back onto the garden beds as finished compost in a matter of months. It was so satisfying to spread that damp, dark brown, crumbly soil around the tomatoes and cucumber vines, knowing that I was nourishing my plants and at the same time saving on the garbage bill. I felt like an alchemist, turning kitchen waste and leaves into black gold.

My part was small—making the pile, turning it occasionally, and spreading it around. The earthworms and potato bugs helped out, along with the rain and sun. The garden lets us join with nature to create. Without us tending them, there would be no gardens, and without the mysterious process that makes seeds spring to life and buds form, we'd have no gardens to tend.

The garden is so generous in its returns—for a small effort on our part it rewards us abundantly. Think about it. We plant one small tomato seed in a pot, water it, and grow it under fluorescent lights from March until May with occasional boosts of liquid fertilizer. Then it's time to set it outside in a shady place for a few days to "harden off," to get used to being in the great outdoors. Plant it in the sun, stake it, keep it watered and fertilized, and your visible rewards are enormous—bushels of tomatoes with soul-satisfying flavor, the kind you can't buy in a store.

The unexpected rewards are greater: spending time outdoors in the sun, rain and dew; listening to the jays and squirrels argue; sharing homegrown grapes with a neighbor; eating honey-sweet figs fresh from the tree; discovering that tomato leaves smell pungent and dye your hands yellow.

When I tromp around in the garden long enough, digging in the dirt, turning it over, weeding on my knees and crawling around on the ground, I begin to know that I am just another tomato seed, part of the whole big cycle of nature, here to become the tomato plant I am and to bear the best fruit I can. I have my own particular nature, just as each plant does.

The gardening process itself slows me down and gives me roots on earth. I touch the ground and begin to feel the mysterious power of life. This is where dirt, seeds, water and sun work together, where shoots, stems and flowers spring up and unfold.

When I brush against the damp leaves of heavenly bamboo, get pricked by the rose thorns, smell the lilies and listen to the wind, my senses come back to life. 'Apricot Beauty' tulips wake up my eyes to the pleasure of color. Hosta leaves alone make me notice how many shades of green there are. There is simply so much to pay attention to in the garden that everyday cares drop away, irrelevant in the face of all this beauty.

Opening Your Heart

One of the most delightful things about gardening is the
freemasonry it gives with other gardeners, and the interest and
pleasure all gardeners get by visiting other people's gardens. We
all have a lot to learn and in every new garden there is a chance
of finding inspiration—new flowers, different arrangements or
fresh treatment for old subjects.

—Margery Fish

OPENING YOUR GARDEN to strangers is the fastest way to make new friends. Like-minded gardeners will recognize you as a kindred spirit. Their pleasure and appreciation for the unique way you've painted with plants will kindle understanding, camaraderie and best of all, that ultimate joy—plant swapping. One highlight of my open gardens over the years was the day a visitor came toward me on the path, enveloped me in a big hug and said: "This is so wonderful!"

Like a lot of new adventures, opening your garden for the first time will both thrill and terrify you. But I promise that once you get over your fear you'll want to do it again and again. Besides making new friends who love what you love, you'll teach and learn, give and receive, and get to share your passion.

Forget about waiting until your garden is perfect—that day will never come. Besides, it will just make everyone else feel inadequate—they'll tour your perfect garden and want to creep home and blow up their own yard. You don't want to cause that kind of misery. Better to leave some stray dandelions and a few unplanted pots lying around. Visitors will be relieved and feel more at

29

home. "It's such a relief to see that your garden has weeds and isn't finished," they'll say. "I feel so much better about my own hodgepodge."

Of course you will want to make it as wonderful as you can, for after all, opening your garden is a chance to complete those projects that have been lingering on the shelves of your imagination. Time to paint the garden bench, fill the feeders, and scrub out the birdbaths. Float a few roses in the fresh, glistening water while you're at it. Prune the water sprouts off the old apple tree, then use them to build a teepee trellis for that clematis that's falling all over itself. (It's easy—just poke five or six straight long branches in the ground at a slight angle and tie them together about a foot below the top with twine.)

Rip out that shady bed filled with Bugleweed that you've always hated, and start over. Enrich the soil with mushroom compost. Splurge on some raspberry astilbes for June and cobalt blue willow gentians for August, and edge the bed with Lenten roses (*Helleborus orientalis*) that will bloom luxuriously next winter.

The week before your open garden invite all your gardening friends over for a cleanup party. Have plenty of tools and gloves on hand. While you're weeding, take along a shallow basin filled with soil to heel in those seedling lady's mantles and cranesbills that you're yanking out but hate to throw away. Pot them up and give them to your friends to take home. Save any extras for guests at your open garden—visitors love to go home with a little piece of your garden that will remind them of their outing. Pass-along plants are a sure way to start a new friendship.

As you deadhead and weed and talk about plants and nurseries and gardens to visit, the time will fly and the garden will shine. Treat your guests to a festive picnic lunch in the garden. Promise to divide or propagate anything they covet—after the open garden—this isn't the time to leave holes in the borders. Keep a little list in the garage so you remember to collect seed of the wine-colored Sweet William for Sally and the unusual dark pink angel's fishing rod for Andrew.

When you send out open garden invitations, ask your guests to wear their garden hats. This will make the day more festive and turn the event into a party. Have a few extra bonnets on hand for those who forget so that everyone can get into the spirit. Fill a big cooler with iced tea and a wicker basket with crisp cookies. No, you don't have to bake—there isn't time, and besides, that will just generate more envy. Put your tools away, throw your jeans in the hamper and slip on your favorite long, flowing dress. Add a big straw hat with flowers on the band, and prepare to have a fantastic day.

Quiet Contemplation

On some winter day when the sky and the

landscape are achromatic I find the garden at its best.

Everything is latent; there is an undertow to the garden

and I sense that below my feet is the whole of summer.

Not the one that is past but the summer to come;

when as yet there is no need to face disenchantment.

—*Mirabel Osler*

WINTER IS A WAITING time. When furry gray magnolia buds sit patiently on their branches, I picture the satin white petals that will unfold next spring and can almost smell their perfume. When small buds like buttons adorn the uplifted branches of the dogwood tree I remember past years' pink blossoms and sigh with longing. I know I must wait until April for real flowers, but meanwhile I see with the eyes of my imagination. This is the way of a gardener, always looking back, always looking forward, and seeing four seasons of change with only twigs in front of her eyes.

Yet there is still beauty to contemplate in the winter garden, quieter than spring's exuberance, summer's lushness and autumn's fire. Winter pleasures come from details that might go unnoticed in fuller times. Ten-foot-tall *Rosa Murielle*, a densely twiggy shrub with modest white flowers in spring, earns its keep in winter with red hips like strings of Christmas lights. *Rosa glauca* too is covered with hundreds of red hips where pink flowers bloomed last spring.

Down in the bog three tall cattails stand proudly in brown velvet coats. One has burst its seams like an old sofa and a cloud of beige seeds hangs suspended, ready for takeoff on the next strong wind. Nearby sits a clump of water iris, its wiry flower stems topped by dark brown seed pods. I like to watch the stems sway as small sparrows perch to feed.

On an impulse, I grab my gathering basket, the same one I use in the summer to collect roses and asters for the house. It will be fun to see what I can find for bouquets in this quiet season. Moving slowly around the garden, I search for interesting leaves, seed pods, berries and dried flowers.

Mexican orange's glossy green leaves are as shiny as if they had been waxed. They smell like citrus when they're cut—grapefruit comes closest to the slightly bitter, fruity fragrance. Silver 'Powys Castle' artemesia glistens in the winter sun. It too has a distinctive scent—pungent and, I'm sorry to say, almost unpleasant. For relief I run my fingers through 'Arp' rosemary which has grown vigorously against the south side of the house for eight years now, through mild and icy winters. I cut a few stems for the house, savoring its minty fragrance.

Moving toward the shadiest part of the garden, beneath the huge old deodar cedar, I spot the shiny leaves of Japanese aralia (*Fatsia japonica*) shaped liked big green hands, only these have seven fingers. I cut a few leaves for the basket—they will make a sturdy base for an arrangement in a wide bowl. Some leather fern fronds, fresh as parsley, will add a touch of lace to my bouquets.

On the north side of this house where it's shady most of the day, I find dwarf sweet box (*Sarcococca hookeriana humilis*) with dark green tapered leaves still holding black berries from autumn. Clusters of pale green flower buds perch along the stems, bringing back a memory of last February's sweet perfume. I can hardly wait for the fragrance to catch me by surprise some sunny day later this winter.

Turning a corner, I see dwarf variegated boxwood brightening the gray day. This plant cheers my heart—its small dark green leaves are outlined in creamy yellow, bringing light into the shade. By some miracle each leaf has a partner exactly opposite it on the branch, so that they look like hundreds of wings. The soothing symmetrical pattern hints of larger ones.

Adding a few stems of variegated boxwood to my basket, I move toward the house, preparing to leave the garden. A few last details catch my eye. 'Carmen' sedum has cinnamon-colored seedheads now—in August its flowers looked like pink broccoli. Astilbe's once-red flowers are dried to the color of nutmeg. And giant Florida grass (*Miscanthus giganteus*) sports tall fluffy plumes the color of wheat. Always changing, buds to flowers to seed pods, the garden is full of glory even in this quietest season.

Ambivalence in Autumn

The sense of rush and urgency that we felt in

gardening last spring is absent now. . . . Autumn is a

time of sweet disorder and permissible procrastination.

—Allen Lacy

"LOOK AT ME!" shouts the Eastern dogwood, all dressed up for fall in brilliant red leaves. "Me too!" calls the bright yellow grape vine, lighting up the top of the arbor. Thick clusters of purple grapes hang below the golden leaves, wafting a delicious scent. Garlands of porcelain berry vine scrambling along a fence line glitter with purple and turquoise berries. 'Flame' willow flaunts orange branches beside the golden stems of 'Bud's Yellow' shrub dogwood.

'Dawn' viburnum hastens to catch up with its showier companions, green foliage flushing burnished burgundy. Flower buds sit just beneath the leaves, waiting to open pink in December. It's as if the entire garden were collaborating in an effort to offset the gray skies and chilly weather with glowing foliage, sumptuous fruit, and surprisingly late flowers.

It's a bittersweet time for gardeners. We bargain for just a few more sunny days to bask in the milky autumn sun, for just a few more dry days to revel in the freedom of jeans and t-shirts before donning the inevitable rain gear and rubber boots. Sometimes we hold on so tight to the joys of summer that the pleasures of autumn take us by surprise.

Like the damp earth, so easy to dig in, now that it's softened by intermittent rain. It's a joy to sink a spade into soil that yields instead of picking away with a mattock at hard, summer-baked clay. Now I can loosen the ground around enormous clumps of Siberian and Japanese iris that haven't been blooming well, lift them and divide them into more manageable chunks, then replant them. It's even possible to knock the loose dirt off the roots and return it to the bed instead of leaving jagged craters behind.

Now it's easy to dig ample holes for transplanting roses on a cool fall morning. I see the results of adding compost to this bed for ten years and exult. The soil is brown and crumbly, a triumph over the original gray clay that threatened to cement the spade to the ground. I remember the horrible sucking sounds the shovel made when I pulled it out of that glop. Change comes slowly in the garden, but with persistent effort, it comes.

I treasure each flower that blooms in autumn because there are fewer. The last roses seem to have stronger perfume now than in summer. 'Madame Isaac Pereire' makes me swoon, and 'Mary Rose' is so fragrant in November—I could swear she had no scent at all in June. Colors too seem more vibrant. The single flowers of 'Red Coat' look radiant in the autumn light, and the shiny red hips of 'Scabrosa' seem to glow.

In the farthest corner of the garden the bright yellow flowers of Maxmillian's sunflower beckon. Ten feet tall, it winds between the branches of the bosc pear tree and leans against the rustic fence. This lanky creature rises up all summer and fall, as if lured by a snake charmer's flute. In October yellow sunflowers with black centers burst into bloom. They cover the stems and telescope upwards, new buds opening every day for weeks. Nearby *Gymnaster savatieri* opens hundreds of tiny pale blue flowers. I impulsively sent for both these plants from a mail order catalog specializing in wildflowers and was pleasantly surprised. Both have survived serious flooding, clay soil, slugs, horsetail, and buttercup—they're my kind of perennials.

Yet another late beauty, *Schizostylis coccinea*, shows off coral flowers from the front of the border as if to say the gardening season will never end. Emerging from plain grassy leaves, the flower spikes look like miniature gladioli and bloom heartily from late summer through late fall. They're like autumn's fiery leaves, offering a grand finale of warmth to thrill and comfort us before winter draws a curtain on the show.

The Luxury of Bouquets

Nature will bear the closest inspection. She invites

us to lay our eye level with her smallest leaf,

and take an insect view of its plain.

—Henry David Thoreau

I'M NOT RICH if you measure my net worth, but I feel like a queen when I cut myself a bouquet. On the table a yellow and white flower arrangement fills the dining room with light, and if I look out the window, I can see the very same plants arranged in the border, so that they mirror each other. But in the purple vase that looks like an eggplant, I can study the flowers close up and soak in their beautiful details. It's June, and the vase is filled with fragrant white mock orange, yellow *Phlomis russeliana,* chartreuse lady's mantle and white Spuria iris.

The Spurias are among the last irises to bloom in the garden, and they look like they're about to take flight. Three slender white petals stretch outward and upward; the remaining three flare downward and are marked with yellow. When you touch them, they feel like satin. Each flower has a tight new bud nestled beside it like a lover, waiting to bloom when its companion fades.

The white and yellow Spurias were the beginning of the bouquet—they were growing to the side of a large, shrubby St. John's Wort where I would hardly notice a few missing flowers. Did I mention that I'm stingy about cutting flowers from the garden? In a vase they will last only a few days, but in the garden they will bloom for weeks, and it's hard for me to justify shortening their lives.

But more and more I am abandoning this frugality

in favor of celebrating the lush opulence of flowers seen up close. After all, I might not get around to seeing every flower, since my garden spans two-thirds of an acre. But the truth is emotional, and as most emotional truths go, it outweighs intellectual considerations. The delight of arranging just the right colors together, the enormous pleasure that these bouquets bring to me and my friends who sit at the table, and the fragrance that greets us when we enter the house all conspire to make me continue this practice of cutting flowers.

Out in the garden, I'm too likely to become distracted. One moment I'm marveling at the sight of the elevator plant's (*Phlomis russeliana*) amazing tiers of yellow flowers, when the sudden sight of a morning glory vine throttling a rose sends me on a mission to untwine the villain and dig it out. Tranquil contemplation of beauty vanishes as adrenaline propels me into action. In the house, I can regard my flowers in perfect peace.

A botanical encyclopedia tells you that *Phlomis* has "verticillasters." It describes them so technically that you must look it all up in a glossary, and soon you're drowning in a barrel of obscure words. But if you cut a flower and put it in a vase, you will see that each butter-yellow blossom is whorled around the stem like a little kid climbing a rope, and that three or more flowers are stacked in layers along the stem like a wedding cake. Each flower has a dozen little turtle beak petals arranged in a perfect circle, and the whole marvel sits perched on a green pincushion with a pair of leaves flaring out beneath like wings. Two little leaves stick out at the top of each uppermost flower like a cowlick. Who dreamt this up?

As complex as *Phlomis* may be, that's how straight-forward are the blossoms of mock orange. Each white flower has four petals surrounding a sprinkling of yellow stamens. Clusters of these flowers explode all along the woody branches of mock orange in June, fresh and white and deliciously fragrant. For me, it's the scent that makes mock orange earn its keep, for the upright and ungainly shrub, with plain green leaves and branches that point every which way, offers no beauty. In a bouquet, the perfume is even more seductive than in the garden, inviting you to inhale every time you pass through the dining room. The yellow stamens echo the yellow markings on the Spuria iris, the yellow petals of *Phlomis*, and the yellow-green haze of lady's mantle.

In the garden, lady's mantle is a mass of greenish-yellow flowers edging the front of the border. The tiny flowers go unnoticed compared to more flamboyant peonies and irises—they translate into a misty veil, a haze of lime, a puff of yellow smoke. In a vase, you can see that each stem has many little branches, with hundreds of tiny star-shaped flowers exploding at the tips. In a bouquet, this branching pattern is perfect for filling in the gaps between larger irises, mock orange and *Phlomis* flowers. It's lady's mantle that knits individual flowers into an arrangement. Even the color is perfect, blending the green of leaves with the yellow of the *Phlomis* and iris petals. Subtle and subservient to the more glamorous flowers, lady's mantle is the quiet friend that brings the circle of prima donnas together.

Cutting flowers brings the garden into the house and lets me play with plants on a small scale, like tinkering in a doll's house. To me, it's a relaxing way of relishing beauty indoors, where concerns about weeding and pruning are at a safe distance. It's also the ultimate luxury. I grew up in New York City, where buying a single stem of flowering quince at the corner florist was a special treat saved for Friday afternoons, to celebrate the arrival of the weekend. Every day becomes a holiday when I can cut flowers for the table and arrange them with all the pleasure of an artist at her palette.

Roses in Winter

If you want me to remember you, give me plants.

—Elaine Hutson

THE FIRST TIME I LAID EYES on the Lenten rose (*Helleborus orientalis*) I was on a dig and rescue mission. My gardening buddy Phil called me up with exciting news—an old estate garden that had belonged to a plant hybridizer was being bulldozed for a housing development. Chances were good that valuable plants still remained in the ground. We raced out together that June day, rumbling along in Phil's ancient Dodge van, which was completely stuffed with empty cartons and a couple of sturdy shovels.

Huge clumps of dark green plants with bold, lobed leaves grew beneath big oak trees. We dug as many as we could, filling box after box with our heavy booty. Late that afternoon and long into the summer evening, we had planting parties at each of our gardens and watered the salvaged plants thoroughly. They wilted a little, but in just a few days they settled into their new homes.

The following February I realized what treasures we had rescued. Pink and cream-colored flowers, some plain and some splashed with maroon speckles, burst into bloom in the middle of winter. They flowered until May, when they formed interesting seed pods. The next year I found colonies of seedlings under the mother plants—all those seed pods had exploded and germinated. With so many plants to play with, I experimented and discovered that Lenten rose prefers shade, but tolerates sun if watered faithfully. It even flowers in dry shade if watered regularly during its first year. Strong deep roots that look like claws make it a survivor.

41

With a four-month-long bloom period and evergreen leaves, Lenten rose is a perfect perennial for the entry garden. I grow it as a warm welcome near my shady front porch together with 'February Gold' daffodils and purple Juliana primroses. It also blooms under a pink 'Dawn' Viburnum that faces my kitchen window—and it makes doing the dishes much more pleasant. The hand-shaped leaves of Lenten rose look great beside the heart-shaped leaves of bishop's hat (*Epimedium rubrum*), another evergreen shade-lover with pink flowers that bloom in spring.

I once saw a forty-foot driveway edged with Lenten roses—imagine the thrill of arriving home to such a spectacular sight on a winter day. But even a modest display is a pleasure. A friend who lives in a condominium grows Lenten roses in big containers near her front door where she can enjoy them every day.

Beyond the Lenten rose, several other species of hellebore are sturdy plants to brighten winter gardens. Bearsfoot hellebore (*Helleborus foetidus*) has attractive dark green leaves in the shape of a pinwheel and pale green flowers edged with a distinctive touch of red. This plant self-sows easily, forming generous colonies beneath deciduous trees. A stand of it blooms in winter under my old apple tree—accompanied by Mrs. Robb's spurge (*Euphorbia robbiae*), which blooms a little later—heralding spring with its bright yellow bracts.

Tallest of the hellebores, the Corsican species (*Helleborus argutifolius*) has clusters of pale green, cupped flowers that open in February and last for months. The leaf margins are zigzagged as if someone had taken pinking shears to them. I like their prickly look—it adds texture to the garden. Give this hellebore shade and a little shelter by placing it near a porch or under a tree. Winter winds and summer heat can be hard on its leaves, blackening or scorching them.

Hellebores are very easy to grow. Add a shovelful of finished compost to new planting holes and water the plants generously during their first year. Top-dress older clumps with more compost, which nourishes the plants and turns the ground below them into a nursery bed. The dark, damp compost is the perfect place for seeds to sprout. It makes it easy to dig out young seedlings whenever you're ready to transplant them or pot them up for friends.

Hellebores are the perfect pass-along plants, so sturdy that you can give them away knowing they will settle down easily into another garden. Your friends will remember you every winter when their flowers light up the borders. If you don't already have some, find a friend who will share a few seedlings and get you started. Don't spend another winter without the company of hellebores. They're great consolers, bringing light to a dark season.

Falling in Love

Once More with Feeling

But green fingers are the extensions of a verdant heart.

A good garden cannot be made by somebody who has not

developed the capacity to know and to love growing things.

—Russell Page

ONE NIGHT I WAS SITTING UP in the balcony at a chamber music concert. I could hear the music but I couldn't see the musicians' faces. I felt so cut off by being far away from the stage that I found a closer seat after intermission.

Now I could see the musicians and it made all the difference. Every so often the violinist would shoot a glance at the cellist and smile, and you could feel their pleasure in playing together. During the saddest movement the violinist kept his eyes closed the entire time. His brow furrowed, his jaw clenched, his mouth squinched tight, and you could see the agony all over his face. The cellist's ordinarily beaming countenance became somber as the plaintive sounds of the strings and piano filled the hall.

When I can see all the details as musicians perform and watch the expressions on their faces I feel much more connected to the music and its mood. The feeling comes through. And even though you can't witness the process of a garden being made the way you can watch music-making at a concert, still, in some gardens the emotional atmosphere is much more evocative than in others.

I believe that these gardens have been tended with passion. Hope of making a beautiful place. Frustration with horrible soil and unfriendly weather. Perseverance, even when plants get knocked over by wind and grazed by slugs. Love of beautiful plants, and the vision to place them in relationship to one another so that a picture emerges far greater than the sum of the parts, a composition as moving in its own way as a quintet for piano and strings.

For in blending the plants comes the greatest artistry in the garden. You must allow each individual to grow in good health, let its unique characteristics shine as clearly as the sound of the violin, yet place it in harmony with its companions so that rich chords sound instead of single notes. Each plant enhances the other and magnifies its beauty when placed well, so that the colors echo one another and create lovely overtones; so that the leaves complement each other and form an overall pattern. Vertical shapes that recur set up a rhythm like staccato notes. Repeated hues and groupings are like familiar refrains in a melody—when the same plants reappear in another part of the garden their familiarity is comforting and unifying.

Just like music, the garden is always in motion and constantly changing. In the concert hall we accept this with better grace. When the music is sad, we flow with the sadness; when the tempo picks up and gains momentum, we sway in sympathy; when the mood lifts, we smile. We'd be wise to do the same in the garden— allow the changes to unfold, experience the feelings, and pass through. Roses will bloom and fade; peonies will rise, then keel over from the weight of blossoms soaked with rain.

Our joy is in tending, even when circumstances are difficult, just as musicians play well even when the lights are hot, even when a string breaks, or a wrong note sounds. Gardening is not a solo performance, for we collaborate with weather and wildlife, with soil and seasons. We are limited by the strength and endurance of our own mortal bodies and the time allowed for gardening, which is never enough. Still, we play on, doing our best and playing with feeling.

The Pleasures of Weeding

The best thing about solitaire is, it's so solitary. . . .
You're allowed to think these aimless thoughts
and nobody asks what you're up to.

—Anne Tyler

WEEDING IS MY SOLITAIRE. To the outside world it looks like I'm working, digging up dandelions and tweaking out cress seedlings, but for me it's a way to relax and let my mind ramble. I think about last night's conversation and appreciate anew some nugget of wisdom a friend shared, or I laugh to myself, remembering a particularly funny story. I feel the sun's warmth on my hair, the grit of soil against my fingers, and catch a whiff of honeysuckle blooming nearby. A patch of white scilla under a big shrub rose makes me wonder how it traveled all the way from the front yard. I know I never planted it there. And where did that golden feverfew come from, or that blue love-in-a-mist? Should I let it grow or pluck it out? Free to drift, my mind meanders between weeding and plans to improve the border, between philosophical reflections and the grocery list. No rhyme or reason, just awareness of light, weeds, worms, soil, breeze, scent, birdsong, and stream of consciousness.

As I trace the long thick roots of morning glory, gently tugging to pull as much of its length as possible, I reflect on the tenacious nature of weeds. At first I hate them for choking my plants, for invading my territory, for growing so quickly. Didn't I just root out the morning glory last week, yanking out reams of it all the way back to the neighbor's fence? How did it return so quickly, and travel so far? Reluctantly, I find myself marveling at its

48

persistence, at the way it sneaks into my garden by slinking underground for yards before springing up in the middle of a rose bush. How clever the way morning glory winds around the stems of the cutleaf elderberry, camouflaging itself all the way up to the top when, uh-oh, the big white flowers give it away. These sumptuous, chalice-shaped flowers are actually so beautiful that Georgia O'Keefe painted them and they stand framed in a museum for the public to admire. Copies of this painting grace millions of wall calendars and posters. If morning glory tendrils wouldn't throttle the entire border, I would let them have their way and enjoy the gorgeous white trumpets right in my own garden.

It's the same with blackberries. When August comes along and the delicious scent of sun-warmed blackberries floats through the back border, I'm glad that a few canes escaped my vigilant eye and fruited along the fence line. But to leave them alone would be to turn my back on the rest of the garden. Blackberries know no bounds and would soon fling their canes into the perennial beds, rooting down and running amuck. I make a note to myself to return in September and dig out the canes. There will never be a shortage of blackberries, for the birds will drop seeds that will start next year's crop, and the whole cycle will recur, despite my best efforts.

There is never an end to weeding. As long as there are seeds and wind, birds and sun, soil and rain, there will always be more weeds. Even the most devoted gardeners become overwhelmed by the relentless nature of weeds. Like cutting onions or sweeping floors, weeding is a repetitive job without glamour or prestige. And yet its rhythm is curiously comforting, like the tirelessly rolling surf. Weeding is satisfying too—you don't have to think, and the results are soon visible. In an hour you can clear a bed of cress so that the cultivated plants shine, and there on the tarp lies a mountain of weeds ready to be hauled to the compost pile.

Like the seasons that unfold in predictable ways, weeds come along in their own order. First cress in the cool, damp winter weather, then dandelions as spring warms the ground, then morning glory and thistle for summer. Autumn brings those weird red and green weeds that splay themselves out along the paths like little mats, and tall goldenrod and dock.

My favorite way to weed is on my knees, hunting for small intruders that hide between perennials and shrubs. It's an excuse for crawling around in a garden of sensual pleasure. That's where I'm free to inhale the damp aroma of loamy soil and brush my fingers against lamb's ears soft as suede. Small ants parade across the noses of tightly closed peony buds, gathering nectar. I come across the first peony flower that has opened, with petals as delicate as feathers.

Weeding is a gardener's meditation practice, a time for wool gathering, a way to become part of the garden as much as the plants and the ants. It's a way to return to childhood when senses were stronger and everything was fresh and full of wonder. Much as I complain about weeds, they give me a chance to explore and experience my garden in the most intimate way.

Giving and Receiving

A stroll around my garden is a bit like the
telling of the rosary, with each bead a friend
remembered by a plant they gave me. . . .
—Pamela J. Harper

IT WAS ONE OF THOSE DAYS. At 4 a.m. the cat threw up on
the rug, at 7 a.m. the smoke alarm went off when I burnt
the toast, and at 10 a.m. my neighbor revved up his chain
saw. I stepped outside to get the mail and noticed that
'Blanc Double de Coubert,' a double white rugosa rose,
had opened overnight. I stepped closer to get a whiff, put
my nose inside the silky petals. Mmmm. I carefully pulled
off a few young stems, grasping them gently to avoid the
bristles. I picked a few clove-scented cottage pinks to add
to my bouquet.

Back inside, I took the pink blown-glass pitcher from
the kitchen shelf, where it's saved for special occasions,
and filled it with water. I held the flowers upside down to
rinse them off and watched green spit bugs swim down
the drain. That's when I noticed the roses are not actually
white but blush pink, that the tiny leaves surrounding
the bottom of each flower are just like the prongs on
a diamond ring. 'Blanc Double de Coubert' has shiny
green foliage that's pleated, as pretty as a fern. I slipped
the roses into the vase with the cottage pinks tucked at
the edges. It was becoming a much better day.

I got to thinking about where 'Blanc Double de
Coubert' came from—my friend Loie Benedict's garden.
I remember her every year when it blooms. Years ago I
visited her garden in Auburn, Washington and admired

this fragrant, fresh-looking rose. Just as I was leaving, Loie grabbed a shovel and dug out a rooted cane. She slid it into a plastic bag and warned me to keep an eye it—this rose was likely to run. But I liked the idea of it running. Actually for my part it could gallop. At that time my garden was a blank slate with plenty of room. Since then 'Blanc Double de Coubert' has spread herself out, but only moderately, because neighboring old roses on their own roots have also been romping beside her. They're all snuggled up together now, an entire bed of wall-to-wall old roses with an underplanting of cranesbills and an edging of lavender.

The other roses came from a friend who was dismantling an old garden some years ago. Dug up and whacked way back, the shrubs arrived at my driveway one dismal February day, looking like dead branches. But that spring and summer, they burst into bloom, wafting sweet scent all along the front path. They turned out to be 'Madame Hardy,' a white Damask rose with charming green button eyes; voluptuous 'Great Maiden's Blush,' flaunting large pastel pink flowers; and velvety red 'Alain Blanchard' that looks like water-stained silk.

These days I'm the one rooting around for canes to give away. My thirteen-year-old neighbor and friend Gavin Younie had been eyeing 'Blanc Double de Coubert' with admiration.

"Can I pick some, Barbara?" he asked. "They're so fragrant!"

"Sure," I said, through clenched teeth. I can be stingy about cutting flowers—they last so much longer in the garden. Gavin has tried to teach me the pleasure of cutting flowers for bouquets, but I'm a slow student, still resisting. Wait a minute—didn't I just cut a bouquet this morning for myself? How can I say no?

"I'd like to dry some of these roses," he said. "I know,

you don't want me to cut too many. I'll take them from the back side of the bush, don't worry."

"Let's see if we can get you a start for your own garden," I said. "That's how I got this plant in the first place—it was a runner from my friend Loie's garden. She's got a beautiful, old-fashioned garden in Auburn, Washington."

We crawled around carefully under the prickly shrub but couldn't find a likely runner. Vigorous cranesbills covering the ground obscured the rose's root system.

"Let's propagate a shrub for you from a cutting," I suggested. "We'll do it in July, when the new growth is as thick as a pencil, yet still flexible. And while we're at it, we might as well propagate some of these other beauties—'Madame Hardy' and 'Hansa'—they're both gorgeous and very fragrant."

We garden to receive, we garden to give. When one little cutting produces a jungle, sharing is easy. When flowers open, the excitement that arises spills over and demands to be shared. I can't bear to have a tree peony in bloom without calling up my friends to bear witness. Imagine a flower the size of a cereal bowl, with petals like swan feathers streaked with pink swirls.

I telephoned my friend Anita and left an urgent message on her voice mail.

"You've got to come over today and see the tree peony before it gets wrecked by the next rainstorm—or maybe it'll be hail this time."

When she called back, I could tell from the static she was on her car phone.

"I'll swing by right after work," she said. "I've got a flat of heliotrope for you that I found at a nursery yesterday—it's purple and fragrant—the whole van smells like vanilla."

"I can't wait!" I shouted. "And you'll have to see

the 'Chilled Wine' Siberian irises when you come over. They're your colors, a blend of raspberry sherbet and navy blue Italian plums."

My friend Jane throws a party every year when her 'Charles de Mills' rose blooms. If you saw 'Charles de Mills' you'd have a party too. This gallica rose has enormous deep purplish-pink blossoms with an old-fashioned look. Each flower unfolds to show a flat face with four symmetrical compartments.

"I love the peace and quiet in my garden, especially after those hectic years raising a big family," Jane explained. "Solitude feels luxurious now, a chance to think my own thoughts quietly and discover what's inside. But there comes that point where you want to shout with joy at the beauty that the garden returns to you—then it's time for a celebration."

"I know exactly what you mean," I replied. "Just the other day, I was cleaning up some old leaves and came across this strange, rubbery newt, all wet and shiny. We stared at each other for a while and breathed together, the newt and I. But then I went across the street to find my neighbor Wes, who's crazy about amphibians. I just had to show him that amazing sight."

You never know what you'll find in the garden, or when. It's full of memories, surprises and discoveries. It's spacious enough to hold the past, the present and the future. It changes every day, and changes me every time I set foot in it.

Transformation

Yet it is in our idleness, in our dreams, that

the submerged truth sometimes comes to the top.

—*Virginia Woolf*

WHAT LOOKS LIKE devil's food cake, feels like silky cake mix and is made from garbage? You guessed it—compost. All summer and fall I drop grass clippings, leaves, vegetable peelings and spent flowers into the big compost bins near my potting shed until they're stuffed. The piles sit all winter and spring, quietly rotting away. Rain moistens all the materials and packs them down. Earthworms silently slither through and take what they need, adding their castings to the pile. It's usually not until August or September that I get around to poking into the pile to see how things are cooking. Underneath the top layer of leaves and clippings sits a dark stack of moist chocolate cake—soft, crumbly compost that I love to run through my fingers.

For the less earthy gardener, a fork and screen are handy to lift out the treasure and sift it to remove twigs, chunks of rock and whatever coarse material has not yet decomposed. But for me it's a chance to have that mucking-about-in-the-dirt childhood experience that I missed, growing up in New York City. The soft velvety texture of finished compost is pure pleasure to touch, and the fact that it started out as kitchen waste and yard debris makes it that much more of a treasure. To me, transformation is one of life's mysterious miracles, whether it's a thorny branch that gives birth to rose blossoms or a pile of brown pin oak leaves that turns into nutritious mulch. Without any effort at all, what is alive and juicy dies and decomposes. After a while, it turns into a substance that is capable of feeding the very plant it came from. How is this, and what does it say about life?

Thousands of worms like red spaghetti wriggle through the compost as I harvest it and shovel it into garbage cans, saving it for next spring when I'll mix it with perlite for potting soil. When the cans are filled I leave the lids half on and half off so that the worms can escape. Occasionally I shake the worms from the insides of the lids into next year's compost pile, where they burrow happily all winter. Their numbers are vast. Worms appear to be sociable creatures, writhing shoulder-to-shoulder like commuters on the New York subway. They squiggle through the black soil and glisten, doing what they know how to do. No searching for the meaning of life, just living.

I feel very rich. Four garbage cans full of compost, and still there is more in the bin. I fill all the five-gallon pots I can find, then start piling more into the wheelbarrow. I'll mulch all the shrubs that need a winter blanket, making sure they are safely tucked in for the long rest. As I tip the barrow and settle the rich black gold around the woody canes of shrub roses and flowering currant, around the trunks of summersweet and viburnum, it seems that the plants quiver with pleasure. Soon fall's first rains will deliver a drink of compost tea to their roots.

There is plenty of the crumbly compost, so I distribute some under the large clumps of hellebores to feed their winter flowers. Next spring when their seed pods explode, the blanket of compost will serve as a nursery bed, inviting the glistening black seeds that fall to settle right in and sprout. In the garden, you can't have too many hellebores, just as you can't have too much compost.

Floral Prozac

The lotus flower blooms most beautifully

from the deepest and thickest mud.

—*Taro Gold*

SOMETIMES AN ANNOYING CHORE brings unexpected joy in its wake. I had that experience one dreary Monday morning in spring, when it was raining as usual. I was sick of it, wondering what on earth I was doing living in a climate where you have to garden in the mud. Surely this time of year should be sunny and mild—like the springs I remembered from my New York childhood—with blue skies, a light breeze and the scent of lilacs floating on the air. It had been intoxicatingly beautiful on Saturday; for one whole day, a taste of honey, and then starting on Sunday, nothing but dismal drizzle.

Glancing out the window, I noticed a bucket of tools that I'd left out by the potting shed on Saturday, in my foolish belief that sunny days were here to stay. I pictured rust growing along the pruner's blades, on the teeth of the folding saw, on the long-handled loppers. Sighing and muttering, I threw on some sweats, stepped into my rubber boots and headed out to the garden. The path made of recycled wood chips was squishy with weeks of rain. My footsteps made sucking sounds and the corners of my mouth turned down in disgust. When I reached the lawn, the ground was firmer but still very wet—small puddles glistened wherever the ground dipped.

I may have been disgruntled, but the birds were having a field day. This was prime time for worm hunting, and starlings swarmed the lower lawn, bobbing and tugging. A green-headed mallard and his brown mate

57

swam serenely in the small pond, every so often diving for morsels, with their feathery bottoms up in the air. A couple of jays swooped from the apple tree to the grape arbor, flashing blue feathers and screeching.

The apple tree was in full bloom, pale pink flowers dotting the branches that stretched up like a ballerina's arms. In the distance the marsh spurge (*Euphorbia palustris*) glowed neon yellow, and beside it, a big wallflower bloomed its head off with electric purple flower spikes. Forget-me-nots stretched like a blue blanket beneath the newly leafed-out roses, and purple bugleweed and bluebells lit up the garden floor. I soaked it all in. I felt my eyes growing softer, my heart lifting, my steps lightening. A smile bloomed on my face.

Happiness filled me as I gathered up a bouquet for the house. Yellow globeflowers (*Trollius europaeus*) like small roses, and blue forget-me-nots like sprays of tiny stars. Next wallflowers, vivid violet, with so many spikes on one plant that I could pick and pick without any notice. Then bluebells, some blue, some pink, some white. A few lily-of-the-valley for their sweet scent, a couple of columbines with nodding blue flowers like an old-fashioned bonnet, and some 'Chilled Wine' irises.

I brought the tools into the garage and the flowers into the kitchen. Forget-me-not petals sprinkled on the countertop like blue confetti as I arranged the flowers, first in a narrow container that scrunched them too much, and then in a wider one that was just right. The burgundy irises made vibrant accents against the blue, violet, pink and yellow.

A gray spring day had been transformed by flowers that bloom no matter what the weather. How lucky that I went out to the garden for that brief errand—imagine how much I would have missed if it hadn't been for fear of rust.

Fanning the Flames

We look backward too much and we look forward too

much; thus we miss the only eternity of which we can be

absolutely sure—the eternal present, for it is always now.

—William Phelps

EVERY YEAR I BALK as summer ends and fall approaches, resisting the change of seasons. I hate the waning of light and warmth, the browning of flowers and bleaching of leaves. The monotonous drumming of rain on the roof, the gray skies and the biting damp air make me blue.

Until the inevitable day in October arrives when the rain stops, and I look out the window and catch my breath. The trees are on fire. Overnight the Amur maple (*Acer ginnala*) has turned brilliant red, and the grape leaves covering the arbor are the color of lemons. The sassafras tree is marbled orange and yellow—its mitten-shaped leaves wave a joyous greeting. The flowering cherry has darkened to mahogany while the purple smoke tree has brightened to flame orange. The flowering pomegranate and the mulberry tree have both gone bright banana yellow.

This year the Eastern dogwood (*Cornus florida*) glows red. Beneath it dark green rosettes of Mrs. Robb's spurge (*Euphorbia robbiae*) glisten in the rain. Even when the wind sends red dogwood leaves fluttering to the ground, Mrs. Robb sits stately all through the fall and winter, secretly spinning next year's flowering stems. In March, hundreds of round, bright yellow bracts will unfurl, shouting "spring is here at last!"

Beside Mrs. Robb, autumn red Japanese grass (*Miscanthus sinensis purpurascens*) rustles in the wind.

Turning reddish-tan in autumn, it glows as if lit from within. Red switch grass (*Panicum virgatum* 'Rehbraun') is more subtle—its crimson fall color is muted by green. Delicate sprays of tiny, dark red flowers form a cloud above the foliage in late summer and fall. These cut nicely for bouquets, providing that extra detail that sparks curiosity. Whatever could those intriguing hazy red flowers be? I love to arrange red switch grass with chocolate cosmos, orange montbretia, and silver 'Huntington' artemesia.

Schizostylis coccinea, a perennial that blooms from August through November, always lifts my spirits as the days shorten. Bright red flowers on strong stems blaze at the front of the border like miniature gladioli. I like deep coral 'Oregon Sunset,' medium pink 'Oregon Sunrise,' and pastel pink 'Viscountess Byng' just as much as the original red. Mixed together in a riot of color, they're as compatible as the streaks of red, orange and pink in a sunset.

Behind them, succulent fall-flowering sedums (*Sedum spectabile*) stand strong. Their pink flowers have darkened to terra cotta, as if to store late summer's warmth. 'Prince' and 'Lady in Black' asters with masses of tiny white flowers like baby's breath bloom beside 'Cherry Glow' beardtongues. All this color warms my heart as I relinquish summer's gifts and turn my attention to autumn's offerings.

Paying Attention

*People are turning to their gardens not to consume
but to actively create, not to escape from reality but to
observe it closely. That the world we live in and the
activity of making it are one seamless whole is something
that we may occasionally glimpse. In the garden, we know.*

—Carol Williams

IN JANUARY THE LENTEN ROSES arrive. First comes the liftoff:
plump pink buds rise up on juicy stems. A little warmth and
their friendly faces open, basking in the winter sun. That's
my signal to cut off last year's leaves so the tattered foliage
doesn't detract from the fresh flowers. This year's shiny new
leaves will unfurl soon after the flowers bloom.

Here's the rub—if I rush, it's so easy to accidentally
cut off a flower stem instead of an old leaf. I groan when
I do that. Brand new hellebore blooms don't hold up
in bouquets, so I've wasted a cluster of beautiful winter
flowers through carelessness. "Never again!" I vow, and
promise to slow down and pay better attention.

When I do, gardening becomes a much fuller
pleasure. I trace each leaf stem to its origin to make sure
it bears no flower buds, and snip it off at the base with a
clean cut. Then I carefully remove the litter underneath
the Lenten roses—decaying sweet gum leaves and lurking
slugs, those soft, slimy, gray torpedoes waiting to slither
into the newborn blooms and gobble them up.

Paying attention turns gardening from a chore to
communion. Each hellebore flower, whether pink or
white or burgundy, has a heart of silky yellow stamens.
Some are splashed with burgundy freckles; others are

unmarked. Each flower begins its life as a bud nestled at ground level. Slowly the stems expand and lift the flowers higher each day. As the flowers rise, they open wider to show their beauty more fully, as if they were opening their eyes to celebrate the return of the light.

To me, hellebores announce the resurgence of life in the garden. They're the first brave blooms to color the winter beds, a great consolation in a bleak season. I must have great sweeps of them—all along the shady beds on the north side of the house, underneath the Japanese snowbell tree, on both sides of the front porch, at the base of the 'Dawn' viburnum. I want to see hellebores from every window when I'm inside the house, from every entrance as I come and go.

The more attention I pay to the hellebores, the warmer my heart grows, as if I'm getting a transfusion from them. It is really an exchange, this communion with my Lenten roses. I groom them and make sure the ground beneath them is clean and free of predators. I mulch the cleared beds with compost to feed the hellebores and receive the seeds that will fall to the ground later in spring. The more I spend time in their presence, the more I enjoy their early beauty, which lasts from January all the way to April.

I have photographed my Lenten roses and sketched them too. I noticed how the flowers nod on the stems, so the only way I can see their shy faces is to lift them up gently with one finger. Ideally you should have a little slope covered with hellebores and gaze up into their faces. But for real gardeners it doesn't matter. We get down on our bellies, look up into their amazing countenances and let the rest of the world disappear.

The Honeymoon
Is Over

A Critic Comes Calling

I want to believe that the imperfections are nothing—
that the light is everything—that it is more than the sum of
each flawed blossom rising and fading. And I do.

—Mary Oliver

I WOKE UP at the crack of dawn after a restless night. Christopher Lloyd, the noted English garden writer, had arrived in Portland as a keynote speaker for the Hardy Plant Society of Oregon, and was due to visit my garden. I owned all of his books and had them stacked up on the table for his autograph.

"Why on earth did I agree to have him visit?!" I asked myself. "There's nothing in my garden but forget-me-not and feverfew, foxglove and Jupiter's beard. And weeds!"

I'd been to see his perfect garden, centuries old with mossy stone walls, elegant slate paths and wedding-cake staircases. Even the plants that dared seed themselves into the paving crevices were connoisseur specimens, choice cultivars of *Campanula* and *Verbascum*. Young, muscular gardeners were everywhere—up on high ladders clipping the ancient yew hedges, down on their knees weeding the beds and borders.

I'd been tidying up my garden for weeks, but the weather had been terrible. Continuous Pacific Northwest "liquid sunshine" had produced huge weeds and enormous slugs. Serious rain had pelted the perennials, leaving them sprawled about with gaps in their centers as if a cat had sat down right in the middle.

I saw all the weaknesses in my garden and sighed. Just then I heard the sound of a car rumbling down the gravel drive and realized company had arrived. I took a deep breath and rearranged my face.

Christopher Lloyd stepped briskly out of the car. A tall, ruddy man with a full head of wavy white hair, he wore brown tweeds and an air of authority. I greeted him warmly, and soon we were walking down the path to view the garden.

Most guests entering my garden give an involuntary gasp when they catch their first glimpse of riotous color, but this time there was an ominous silence. Lloyd stopped in front of 'Russell's Cottage Rose,' a fragrant pinkish-purple rambler that was waving its arching canes around in search of support.

"I hate the habit of that plant," he declared.

"Well, the rain hasn't helped," I apologized.

"Oh yes, and if the sun were out, it would be the sun's fault," he shot back.

"Well, I plan to build a little summer house here to give the rose a place to climb, and visitors a place to sit. Next year, as soon as I can take out that old apricot tree that never bears fruit."

"What do you need a summer house for, when you have a perfectly good house that you live in right over there? Why don't you train that rose up the apricot tree? At least it has character."

Because I hate that ugly tree, I thought to myself, smiling at the unwanted advice.

"Do you have problems with mildew and black spot on your roses?" I asked, hoping to divert him from further critiques.

"I did, but I pulled them all out. I'm growing cannas and yuccas instead."

I shuddered at the thought of replacing fragrant, colorful roses with spears of maroon and gray leaves. But what did I know, after all—I'm just an ordinary gardener who loves my flowers, trying to make the best of a wetland on clay soil.

We advanced further into the garden, stopping to look at a long border of Michaelmas daisies and sneezeweeds that turn into an ocean of lavender, pink and yellow flowers every fall. Just the week before I had carefully planted a dozen annual sunflowers in this bed to jazz it up with summer color and bold foliage. The new plants were still small, waiting for some sun to help them grow. I could barely see their leaves peeking out between the neighboring perennials.

"You need stronger leaves in this planting," Lloyd commanded, "better structure. And everything needs a good feed. These plants are too small."

I nodded sagely, veiling my irritation.

He marched forward toward the big summer borders.

"What a splendid patch of yellow iris over there!" he enthused. I smiled, warmed by these first words of praise.

"But you've only got the one patch. You need to repeat it, perhaps another splash of yellow over there, and in that corner—a mullein, or some other plant with good leaves and vertical form."

I hated to admit that bright yellow was my least favorite color, and that the patch of yellow iris was an accident, a mistake, actually. It's such a domineering color, like a traffic sign.

"Have you thought of growing Crambe cordifolia in this garden?" Lloyd queried. "It's quite a lovely plant with big bold leaves."

"Maybe next year," I offered. "Perhaps with some Geranium psilostemon nearby, and some yuccas."

"Yes, now you're getting it!" Christopher exclaimed. I smiled shyly.

"And some cannas over here? With a few bright

yellow mulleins for vertical emphasis?"

"Yes, yes, that's the idea," he agreed. "But I should certainly get rid of this rose first. It's quite terrible. Look how the flowers fade so quickly."

Lloyd was pointing at 'Red Coat,' one of my favorite shrub roses. It blooms from Memorial Day to Thanksgiving, with big single red flowers that I can see all the way from my bedroom window. Until now I'd never noticed just how dingy the older flowers become.

"You'll have me digging up my entire garden before this day is over!" I complained.

"Well yes, one should always be changing," said Christopher, heading for the next bed. "Why I had my head gardener dig out all my roses just a few months ago."

I held my tongue and counted to ten. I had no head gardener—not even an assistant gardener.

"And look over here," he went on. "You need some bolder leaves for contrast, some hostas for example. And why don't you have any ferns in the garden? And for goodness sakes, where are your hydrangeas?"

Totally deflated, I realized with relief that we'd finished our tour of the garden.

"You must come and see me again in England," were Christopher's last words to me, as he autographed the pile of books that I'd stacked up on the picnic table.

It took me days to get over the shock of having my garden assaulted. It was like showing baby pictures only to be told that your precious child had big ears and funny hair.

My visitor was right in theory. Yes, there are standards for excellence in garden design, and it is important to have repetition, structure and contrast. But I love my garden with all its shortcomings. With limited time and money, it'll never be perfect, but it brings me oceans of joy.

I've added some bold-leaved rodgersias and castor beans, and I must admit they do improve the borders. But I love 'Red Coat' even if the flowers fade, so it's staying. As for the summer house, I continue to dream about it. And I still wince at bright yellow. No celebrity on earth is going to talk me into more of it!

Enough Already

Pretty though this bulbous plant (Star of Bethlehem) is when it opens its pure white starry flowers over the deceptively crocus-like leaves, it increases at the root at a phenomenal rate. I spent the next 25 years digging it out, but made practically no impression on it because, for every bulb extracted, at least five minute bulblets dropped off to start lives of their own.

—Graham Stuart Thomas

SMOKE GOT IN MY EYES, but this was no romance. I was standing in front of a dozen brown cattails that were exploding, sending streams of fluffy white seeds my way. I couldn't help seeing the beauty of it, all these silky wisps floating along like clouds, glistening in the soft autumn sun. But at the same time I thought, good grief, where will all these seeds land? Will I find cattails sprouting between my hybrid musk roses next summer, or keeping company with the delphiniums?

Siberian irises have taught me that it's no use being permissive with seedpods. At one time I enjoyed their dark, decorative seedpods in the winter. Chickadees would perch and peck, making the stems sway and rattle. But for every seed they ate, three or four would fall to the earth and sprout. Soon a Siberian iris forest grew, and after years of digging up these muddy-colored seedlings, I decided to cut the seedpods off in the fall. Easier said than done. If I miss just one or two that are hiding in the jungle of iris foliage, dozens of seedlings are in the works.

At least it's easy to dig up irises if you get them while they're young. Sea holly is another story. Their mysterious, thistle-like, blue-gray flowers and strong, silvery stems are anchored by deep white taproots that settle down for good, like long, tenacious parsnips. These roots run underground, sending up colonies of sea holly, but that's not enough. Sea holly also spits its hard seeds at neighboring perennials, sneaking in to sprout between the purple coneflowers and asters that I love, threatening to smother them. So the minute I notice sea holly flowers fading from steely blue to muted gray, off with their heads. I enjoy their color when they're fresh, but won't risk losing a bed of mixed perennials to a sea holly monopoly. I cut off their fading flower stems with a firm, gloved hand, for these unusual plants are prickly to boot.

Although I've held back the tide of sea holly, I'm drowning in *Verbena bonariensis*, a plant that I love and hate in equal measure. It was love at first sight when I encountered it in Faith MacKaness's perennial border out in Corbett, Oregon. The tall branching stems were covered with purple flowers, and wove in and out of the pink plumes of queen-of-the-prairie (*Filipendula rubra*) that flowered beside it. Orange skippers flitted among the purple flowers. I had to have this plant.

"It's a pest, but it's a nice pest," Faith warned me. Still I begged a start. She handed me a few seedlings in a plastic bag, cautioning me to keep an eye on them, or they'd take over my garden. Why do I refuse to learn from other gardeners' experience? I'd have to have eyes all over my head to keep up with *Verbena bonariensis*. Its tiny flowers form seeds like specks of dust that find their way to every bed and border of my garden. No doubt neighbors for blocks around are wondering where this charming tall purple flower came from.

Every fall I cut down thousands of stems of *Verbena bonariensis* that are going to seed, and even as I clip them, millions of seeds drift around in the air. Every spring I pluck thousands of seedlings out of the damp earth. How many hours of my life have I spent orchestrating the growth rate of *Verbena bonariensis*? How much time have I spent watching the orange skippers darting from one purple flower to another? How many stems of delicate purple flowers have I cut as filler for summer bouquets of roses and speedwells?

Garden books will warn you to cut off the seedpods of prolific plants before they seed down so extravagantly. But the window of opportunity is too small. One day, everything in the garden is ripening to fruition, and overnight seedpods in every bed are readying themselves for the big boom. By the time you hear the popping of spurge (*Euphorbia*) seeds, it's too late . . . they've launched themselves hither and thither. Even if a gardener rose at dawn with secateurs in hand, by the time he began to snip in the front beds, seedpods in the back borders would be firing away. Let's face it, it's bigger than the best of us.

Frustration

Prejudice against people is reprehensible, but a healthy set of prejudices is a gardener's best friend. Gardening is complicated, and prejudice simplifies it enormously.

—Allen Lacy

A BIG PART OF BEING a garden designer is paying careful attention to people's tastes and understanding that everyone is different. It's a lot like being a gardener, where learning the unique nature of each plant and what it needs to thrive is so important. Some clients are more challenging than others, and part of my job as a designer is to get a handle on what they want. Sometimes a customer who seems tough at first can be the most rewarding, and I end up learning as much as I teach.

The first time I met Eleanor, she came to the door dressed in a cornflower blue and white print dress and red flats. Her curly white hair was tightly permed.

"Stay in the house, Jasper," she said to the plump dachshund who watched us mournfully from behind the screen door.

"Let's go look at the disaster," she said with an ironic smile. We crunched down the gravel path to the back yard.

"I told that last landscape architect how much I hate pink," Eleanor complained. "But what did she bring? Pink rock daphne, pink azaleas, pink rhododendrons! I just had to throw them out." We were staring at a completely bare bed, erstwhile home of the pink offenders, which were lying at the bottom of a ravine behind a perfectly clipped boxwood hedge.

"Tell me the colors that make you happy," I said.

My mechanical pencil was poised over an old-fashioned brown clipboard as I prepared to take notes.

"White, I love white, but it has to be clear, not pinkish, or yellowed. And blue, but only real blue, like cornflowers. Red, but only lipstick red, not those awful magentas or purplish-reds. And I don't mind a little yellow, as long as it's saturated, not any of those wimpy-looking pale yellows."

I scribbled quickly, keeping my eyes on the clipboard. Oh my, I thought, I had my work cut out for me.

"Let me make sure I understand what you like," I said, struggling to keep a straight face. "It sounds like you want clear primary colors, red, white and blue, with a little yellow thrown in."

"That's exactly right, Barbara. And I want it all to be evergreen. My husband and I look out on this bed year-round from the kitchen, living room and dining room, so I need to have leaves out there at all times."

Oh lord, I thought, next she will tell me it has to bloom in the winter.

"It would be nice to have color all the time, just a little something," Eleanor continued. "And I'd like to be able to cut plenty of flowers for the house, so pick plants that have long-lasting flowers."

"It's going to take me some time to figure it out, but I'm sure I can come up with a good plan," I said with completely false confidence. No sense looking hesitant and weak in the face of the impossible.

"How's the light on that bed?" I asked, hoping it was shady enough for winter-blooming Lenten roses.

"Sunny and baking hot," my client replied. Naturally.

I took my notes home and agonized for a few days. Ideas came to me in bits and pieces, and eventually I designed a plan with mainly white flowers, many good for cutting, and primarily evergreen foliage. There was just one catch—some of the plants were normally shade lovers and would have to be watered faithfully to survive. I figured that Eleanor was determined enough to agree to this condition. And I was right about that. When I proposed my ideas, she was enthusiastic.

"I love to water," she assured me, "and when I'm away, my daughter is very good about it."

What I didn't yet understand was that Eleanor and I perceived color differently.

Next week, after I'd unloaded all the plants and placed them in the bed, Eleanor came out to take a look.

"Oh my, Barbara, I'm afraid those asters will have to go back. They're lavender, and you know I hate anything with pink in it."

"Gosh, Eleanor, to me they look blue. I'll be darned. Well, if you're sure they look lavender to you, I guess they need to go back." She nodded her head yes, and I began to haul the plants back to the wagon.

When I returned to the bed, Eleanor was frowning at the six pincushion flowers.

"I hate to say this, Barbara, but those pincushion flowers are lavender too, or some kind of pale pastel blue. They just don't make me happy."

"What if I trade them in for some white ones?" I asked. "We'll end up with a lot of white in the bed, but that's better than having colors you don't like. And I'll replace those daisies with some true blue delphinium, just as long as you don't mind staking them."

"That's exactly right, Barbara, true blue and pure white. And no, of course I don't mind staking. Richard, the fellow that prepared the soil, can help me with that."

I carried the pincushion flowers back to the car and sighed. Oh well, I'll have a lot of blue in my garden this summer. Or should I say lavender? The more I looked at those flowers, the more I realized they were blue-violet, not true blue. Live and learn.

Eleanor and I worked together that summer and fall, planning a series of perennial beds with definite color schemes: a blue and yellow border with lots of delphiniums and meadow rues, a red and white border full of cardinal flowers and 'Casa Blanca' lilies, and finally a white border in the shade with bleeding hearts and primroses, astilbes, hydrangeas and Japanese painted ferns. I learned a lot more from Eleanor than the difference between blue and lavender.

"I'll bet you think I'm the pickiest person you ever worked with," Eleanor said one day in September, when we were brainstorming about the white border.

"Not really," I said. "For me, it's much harder to work with someone who's wishy-washy. You know what you want and you're not afraid to tell me. Sure, sometimes it's tough to find forty-five varieties of white flowers that bloom non-stop and cut well—but I love a challenge! Besides, it's your garden, and you get to have what you love here."

Eleanor giggled. "I guess I am a white nut—maybe that's what happens in old age—pure white for the soul. Lately, nothing makes me happier than white, so I'm really excited about this new white border. I just loved those white daisies and lilies in the first border we made—I had plenty to cut for the house and for church. And you've introduced me to so many new plants. It's been a real education."

I smiled with pleasure. "Thank you, Eleanor. You've taught me a lot too. I hope I can become as clear as you are about what I want, and as direct as you are about asking for it."

The following spring Eleanor died unexpectedly, in her sleep. Her daughter called to tell me and asked if I'd walk through the garden with her and teach her how to maintain the plants. She planned to stay in the house, at least for a while, caring for her elderly father, who ironically had been failing while Eleanor had been full of life. The garden looked great when I visited, and I thought fondly of Eleanor's pride in carefully arranged color schemes and well-tended plants.

I remember Eleanor in my own garden when orange lilies bloom in front of the red Bourbon rose, and when the salmon daylilies that I keep forgetting to dig out clash with pink 'Bonica' rose. When the bright yellow flag irises seed themselves in front of the pastel pink 'Duchesse de Montebello' rose, drowning out her delicacy and hurting my eyes, I think of Eleanor and her sensitivity to color.

When blinding yellow loosestrife appears in front of pale pink cranesbills, I find myself whispering "I promise I'll take them out, Eleanor, right away."

"Exactly right, Barbara," I hear her reply.

Removing the Rose-Colored Glasses

*Gardeners are the ones who ruin after ruin get on with the high
defiance of nature herself, creating, in the very face of her chaos
and tornado, the bower of roses and the pride of irises. It sounds
very well to garden a "natural way." You may see the natural
way in any desert, any swamp, any leech-filled laurel hell.
Defiance, on the other hand, is what makes gardeners.*

—Henry Mitchell

THE GARDEN IS A DANGEROUS place. I don't know what I
was thinking when I wrote *Garden Retreats: Creating an
Outdoor Sanctuary.* At the time I thought the garden was
a place of refuge. I hate to admit it, but I was wrong. Just
the other day when I was all relaxed, peacefully cleaning
up the garden, a Siberian iris pod punched me smack in
the eye. What a shock! I retreated all right, all the way
back to the house, and poured in the eye wash. I looked
in the mirror and saw an eyeball red as a traffic light. It
was Sunday, and all the doctors were busy in their own
gardens, so I asked my partner Tom to please drive me to
the urgent care center.

The nurse practitioner painted my eye with a
yellow dye and took a peek. "Looks like your cornea is
scratched," she pronounced.

"How bad is it?" I asked. "Is it big?"

Tom peered into my eye. "It looks a lot like the state
of Pennsylvania," he said.

I was given a prescription for antibiotic cream and
instructions to visit my ophthalmologist the next day.

I spent the next morning waiting for the doctor in an office filled with eye patients. Some wore glasses, others had an assortment of afflictions—crossed eyes, lazy eyes, eyes covered with gauze—which made me feel pretty fortunate by comparison. After two hours, the physician's assistant greeted me and took me into the inner sanctum, where he questioned me briefly and left me to wait some more. It was a small office with eyes everywhere. There were charts of healthy eyes and all their parts, and unhealthy eyes with every kind of disease. A large white plastic eyeball sat on a pedestal next to the examination chair. I was surrounded by eyes, with nowhere to go.

I sat on the patient's throne, which looked a lot like the barbershop chairs you see in the old movies, only this one had a gizmo where you rest your chin while the doctor examines your eyes with an assortment of bright lights and scopes.

"Look left, look right, look up, look down," he instructed, as I rolled my eye obediently. Every so often he'd squirt some drops in, or throw in a drop of dye just for a change. He pointed bright lights at my eye, puffed air into it and gave it much more attention than it ever had had. Finally he stopped and rolled his sleeves down.

"OK, we're done with the eye torture for now," he said. "Rest that eye for at least a day—no reading, no gardening, not even any walking outdoors. A slight wind or a speck of dirt is too risky right now. You can watch TV or videos—the eye doesn't have to work as hard staring at a screen as reading lines of print."

As we were wrapping it up, I thought I'd better come clean. "You know, I'm a passionate gardener," I said. "Should I go out and get some goggles to be safe, for later on?" I was asking half in jest, but he told me that right across the street there was a hardware store where I could buy a pair of safety goggles. Sure enough, there were four different models, all inexpensive and sturdy. I bought the wraparound style and tucked them in my purse. On the way home, I stopped at the library and checked out some books on tape and videos.

I spent that evening and the next day resting my eye, soothing it with eye drops and eye cream. My books sat on the table, closed. I could see their colorful covers and could hardly stand it—this was like being on a diet with a big box of chocolates right in front of you. I listened to books on tape, but it just wasn't the same as reading. I watched a video in the middle of the afternoon and felt decadent. I had to replay the doctor's words to keep from jumping up and grabbing a book. "Act as if you have the flu, and just stay put . . . no reading if you want your eye to improve. Otherwise, it will take that much longer."

The next day I went back to the doctor, and after examining my eye he declared that it was healed enough to read, and even to garden. Back home I ate lunch and started a brand new novel, elated to be back to normal. I returned to the garden, slipped on the goggles, and cut back the rest of the irises.

"Take that!" I muttered as I whacked off brown seed pods, including the one that had punched me in the eye. I pruned back some old roses and then hacked a few blackberries that were reaching over my neighbor's fence. I looked like an aviator and felt like a warrior. Besides the goggles, I wore leather gloves to protect my fingers from thorns. I had my trusty Felco pruners and a narrow-nosed trowel holstered to my belt. A sweatshirt kept out the wind, a hooded rain jacket and waterproof boots kept me dry, and sunscreen blocked any rays that might infiltrate the cloud cover.

Each year the garden becomes increasingly dangerous, but I never give up. I've been stung by yellowjackets, torn by thorns, bitten by no-see-ems, and poked in the eye by a seed pod. Just when I think I've protected myself against all harm, up comes another enemy. Still, I try to relax in my garden retreat, by remaining vigilant, enjoying the mostly peaceful atmosphere, yet ready to do battle with the next foe.

Too Tied Down

You become responsible, forever, for what you have tamed.

—Antoine De Saint-Exupery

I TOOK A THREE-DAY break to visit gardens and nurseries up north with my friend Anita. We returned late Sunday night, tired but happy, with memories of fragrant roses, purple clematis, and a bounty of newly-purchased plants that we hadn't been able to resist. But when her red van turned into my driveway, the headlights shone on dozens of wands of white *Gaura lindheimerii* that had ballooned out onto the asphalt, blocking the way.

We unloaded out in the street by moonlight, and I hauled my suitcase up the drive, careful not to disturb the forest of Gaura. I walked back to the road for my two cartons of plants and tripped over a lady's mantle that had seeded itself into one of the small cracks where the asphalt was crumbling.

I got the boxes and set them on a wicker table on the porch, ready to go into the house and call it a night. But when I tried to open the screen door, it was covered over with tendrils—several branches of silver vein creeper (*Parthenocissus henryana*) had plummeted down from their arbor and were twining around the doorknob. I pried them off and made a mental note to retrain them back onto the overhead grid the next morning.

I unpacked and fell into bed, dreaming of where I would plant the hydrangea I'd brought back from Cultus Bay Nursery on Whidbey Island. When I woke up, I decided to throw some laundry into the washing machine before going out to water the garden. As I closed the lid on the washer, I looked up to see that long chains of Kennilworth ivy had threaded their way through tiny

81

gaps around the basement window, and were creeping down the wall. When I opened the basement door to go outside and remove the ivy, I saw that more of it was slinking across the threshold. Spiders had woven a web over the entrance, so I got a chopstick to pry my way out, and, tripping over the ivy, stumbled up the basement steps.

Brilliant white flowers greeted from across the lawn—my neighbor's morning glory had finally made it to the top of their laurel hedge and were flowering in full force, twining their way through the thicket and moving toward my mixed border. I ran across the yard, tiptoed through the border, and started pulling at the long ropes of morning glory. They had wound themselves around each other, forming thick tangles, and I tore off as much as I could of the twisted ropes. Then I headed over to the neighbor's driveway to pull more of it from their side of the hedge. That's when I saw the blackberry that was shooting thorny canes toward the fence, canes that would lengthen and root down and eventually creep under the fence and invade my garden. I whipped my Felco pruners out of their holster and cut the blackberry down to the ground, swearing to dig it out later.

There had been a time when I used to feel sorry for plants for being immobile. They had to stand out there in the pelting rain and icy cold, in the blistering sun and desiccating wind, without any way to escape. Now my whole notion of plants being stationary was beginning to dissolve. They were thugs in motion, compensating for their lack of feet by developing runners and tendrils, sprouting suckers and shooting canes with thorns . . . they were moving in on me and there was nowhere to escape. How could one woman armed with Felco pruners and a trowel hold back the tide? It had been a big mistake to think I could go away for a weekend. You can't turn your back on a garden.

Absence Makes the Heart Grow Fonder

Waiting

Clouds come from time to time—

and bring a chance to rest

from looking at the moon.

—*Basho*

LATE JANUARY and the ground is frozen, the trees are coated with white frost, and all the beautiful little evergreen colonies of Mrs. Robb's spurge are huddled together shivering in the cold. This is a time of stillness. It's the dormant season, from the root *dormire*, meaning "to sleep." I would like to return to my bed and slumber on this Tuesday morning, but instead I bundle up in fleece, sip hot Earl Grey tea, and write, looking out onto the bleak landscape. Even the rake stands against the sweet gum tree in repose, and the compost pile is frozen stiff. Nothing moves in the garden.

So the sight of a few birds flying between the tree tops is a relief of sorts. Life wants to move. So much stillness smacks of death. I long to go outside and do something— my fingers itch for the pruners and the trowel. I want to pull weeds, to prune roses, to grab a handful of lavender and pinch the leaves, releasing the aroma of summer, of love, of happiness. Winter is a hardship, a deprivation, an absence that makes me cranky. But remembering how cold it is out there, and how quickly my fingers will turn red, I decide to be a bear in winter, to hibernate and be still.

This quiet time is part of a cycle that comes each year, a breathing space between all the planting and tending, all the grooming and feeding. It's a time to reflect, to look, to contemplate, to simply be rather than do.

In every life process there's a segment like this. Just before the seed germinates, it sits quietly underground, in the dark, out of sight. A certain amount of faith is required for us to leave it alone under the soil and let it spring to life in its own sweet time. We wait. The same with the bulbs that we bury each fall. Underground they sit for months, invisible to us, doing what bulbs do in the deep of winter, until it is time for them to spread their roots and send their shoots up into the upper world.

And it is the same with us, with our own internal growth processes. We have a knot to unravel, a problem to solve, and we mull, we discuss, we write, we contemplate, and then we bury it in our own sweet unconscious mind and sleep on it. The seed, the bulb must rest a while in the dark, must quiet down before it is ready to send down roots and send up shoots and bloom into understanding. Perhaps a dream will come in the night to cast some light, or an insight will appear some days later. No need to rush or worry—the quiet time, the night, the waiting, are all part of the growth process.

A Way of Life

Biting into an apple

as I sit before peonies—

that's how I'll die.

—*Shiki*

EVER SINCE I STARTED gardening, way back in 1972, I've heard the same refrain from well-meaning neighbors and friends. "Don't work too hard!" said Frank, who lived next door to my first home and garden in Northeast Portland. Frank showed me how to turn over the soil and rake it into a smooth seedbed. That I learned. But when he tried to teach me how to lean on the shovel and take a break, or call it a day at 5 p.m., I balked.

"Don't overdo!" cautioned Megs, my neighbor two doors down from my garden in West Slope. "Come over for a glass of iced tea when you're finished weeding," she urged. "Maybe a little later," I say with a smile. I continue to weed, and before long, I'm completely immersed in the garden.

They just don't understand. For me, gardening isn't work, it's a way of life. Even my idea of a vacation is to go visit gardens. One highlight was a trip to tour the gardens of Scotland and England. At first it was a pleasure to have clean fingernails and relaxed muscles. Taking a break from gardening seemed like a treat, until the day we went to Christopher Lloyd's noted garden, Great Dixter. I was enjoying the sun's warmth on my hair as I leisurely photographed the long border, when a gardener rounded the bend. He was filthy, covered with dirt, his hands brown all the way up to the wrists. I had a pang of longing to be in his muddy boots. Later, approaching the vegetable garden, I watched two young men gossiping as they weeded the onion rows. Eavesdropping from a discrete distance, I itched to kneel down and get my fingers into that soft brown dirt.

Often it was fragrance that made me yearn for my own garden. Outside a castle, pots of variegated geraniums perched on a stone ledge beckoned—I rubbed the leaves and inhaled essence of peppermint. A stand of rosemary bushes three feet tall on the south side of an old English home begged to be touched. I grabbed a handful of branches, releasing the sweet minty scent, and remembered cooking chicken with fresh rosemary from my garden just the week before at home.

When John Findlay, owner of Carnell Gardens, took us through his freestanding greenhouse—or glasshouse as it's called in Scotland—we saw the familiar slimy trails of slugs that had nibbled on his *Streptocarpus* and felt right at home. Fortunately, only the leaves were damaged, and the brilliant blue flowers sparkled in the sunlight. Then he led us through another tall, narrow glasshouse attached to his home and handed each of us a perfect white peach from a tree that he had carefully espaliered against the warm brick wall. Although hard as apples, they were surprisingly juicy and flavorful. That's when I felt a wave of homesickness for my own garden where Fall Gold raspberries would be ripening in the September sun and Concord grapes would be hanging in thick purple clusters from the arbor.

John led us through his musty potting shed where ancient spades, forks, rakes and saws hung immaculately from their assigned nails. A pile of dark brown compost called to me from the potting bench and I plunged my hand in, lifted out the lovely dirt and crumbled it between my fingers. Ecstasy.

I'm back home now and blissfully digging up last

year's composted leaves. I love to run my hands through the crumbly, damp stuff that is halfway between old leaves and new soil. It's rotted enough to spread over the beds as a topdressing and to use as a coarse potting mix for plants that need to go into bigger pots for the winter.

I listen for the sounds of ornamental grasses rustling in the autumn breeze, especially the giant Florida grass that reminds me of bamboo. I can smell the sweetness of slipskin grapes that still dangle from the vines and the vinegary scent of fallen apples and pears dampening the parched ground.

Maybe life is a series of longings, desires to travel when I'm working at home, yearnings to be home when I'm overseas. Maybe distance is needed to appreciate what is so easy to take for granted in everyday life—the details of smell and touch and sound that make the pleasures of gardening so powerful. This fall I love the garden even more after my recent absence.

Wave Hill in the Winter

Summer amplitude, barely recollected, belongs to

some other continent; it's now that counts, when the

garden is deep in hibernating peace.

—Mirabel Osler

GOING BACK EAST to see my family has a few crucial traditions—lots of hugs and kisses, nonstop talking to make up for lost time, and above all, a visit to Wave Hill, an oasis in The Bronx. I stay with my father and stepmother in Riverdale, a short distance from the garden. A glance out the window shows a clear blue sky and blinding sunshine, but it's actually twenty degrees according to the outdoor thermometer on the terrace.

My stepmother Celia will stay home this morning, glad to have the time to catch up with several friends on the phone. For her birthday last year I gave her a pin in the shape of a telephone to signify her love of conversations. She presses a long woolen coat and hat on me, certain that I will freeze to death in my Oregon clothes. I protest, showing her how warm my woolen Peruvian shawl is. She insists that anything that short will not do, and before I know it I'm marching out the door dressed in her long black coat and turquoise velvet hat. My father is outfitted in a long gray coat and a hat with earflaps, which he lowers as soon as we hit the street.

He warms up the old brown Buick, carefully adjusts the mirrors, and we're on our way. The roads on the way to Wave Hill are lined with stately Tudor homes and established gardens with majestic oaks and dramatic rock outcroppings. Soon we pass through brick pillars into the parking lot and I feel a tingle of excitement. Wave Hill has treats at any time of the year, and I wonder what we'll see on this clear, cold January day.

A blaze of yellow winter jasmine greets us—the vines are tumbling over an old stone wall and look like forsythia run amuck. 'Golden Sword' yuccas guard the entry like small sentries, with dwarf blue junipers spread out at their feet. Hellebores huddle nearby, shivering in the cold, their buds tight. I think of my hellebores at home blooming in shades of pink in our milder winter and feel a little smug.

We approach the perennial border and I remember it from summers past, with pink roses and purple butterfly bushes blooming beside lavender Russian sage. Now it is mostly skeletal, with a few dark green yew mounds at the corners of the beds. Fir boughs are piled here and there, protecting tender plants. I count my blessings again that we can grow so much more in Portland without taking such measures.

My father and I are thoroughly frozen by now and decide to thaw out in the conservatory. Cobalt blue flowers that we've never before seen, or even imagined, grab our attention. A gardener tells us they are *Pychnostachys*. A gorgeous hoya with deep wine-colored flowers turns out to be *Hoya macgillivray* 'Superba'—according to the label, it was grown from seed and took four years to flower. I show my father how to taste the glistening hoya nectar and he touches his finger gingerly to the flower, smiling with delight at the sweetness.

Thoroughly warm, we venture outdoors again to check out the trees. An enormous lacebark pine, its gray bark flecked with yellow spots, catches my eye from a distance. A giant beech tree with a trunk like an elephant's leg commands a square block. And glistening in the winter sun, a young golden conifer beckons us. When we get closer I can tell from its long needles in bundles of five that it's a Himalayan pine, and the label notes that it's a special cultivar called 'Zebrina.' Each needle is striped green and yellow, just like zebra grass, making the tree a luminous accent in the winter landscape. I take one long needle for a souvenir.

"Thanks for humoring me while I drag you all around this garden," I tell my father. I'm sure this is foreign to him, and not that interesting. He lives in a high-rise apartment building and grows cacti on the windowsills.

"No, I like it," he says. "You know if I came here without you, all I'd see would be grass and trees. Today I got to taste hoya nectar and see spotted bark and needles in bundles."

I'm tickled to know this. Still, naturally he is ready to leave far sooner than I am. We take a quick look at the pergola overlooking the Hudson river, and I check the bare vines for some hint of what will leaf out in the spring. My best guess is wisteria, ornamental kiwi (*Actinidia kolomikta*) and clematis. If I'm lucky I'll get back in the summer to see the leaves and flowers.

As we depart Wave Hill a big old winterberry (*Ilex verticillata* 'Christmas Cheer') loaded with red fruit brightens a shrub border. Several witch hazels sparkle— twisted ribbons of yellow and orange bloom on the bare branches. I leave walking backwards to memorize a last glimpse of the Hudson river framed by the pergola.

Weekend Away with a Friend

The only form of extended vacations that's really acceptable is to go on a tour of fine gardens elsewhere. Experiencing the gardens of great manicured estates provokes a profound sense of the inadequacy of one's own small efforts and a burning desire to rush home and get to work on a whole new landscape scheme.

—Des Kennedy

WHEN SANDY AND I PULLED into the parking lot at Lewis and Clark College for the tenth annual Hardy Plant Society of Oregon Study Weekend there were few hints of what was going on inside. A woman in a flowery sundress was carrying a full box of plants back to her car, which prompted us to move a little faster.

"Uh-oh, they've already started the plant sale," I panted, struggling up the hill in floppy sandals and a long skirt.

"Let's rush in, throw my sweater across two seats, and hurry out to the sale tables," said Sandy. She raced ahead of me in sensible running shoes and jeans. Sandy is an accountant who always comes up with a practical strategy.

When we got inside, it was not so simple. Tempting flower arrangements sat on the registration tables, begging to be studied. Gardeners were everywhere, shouting "hello" and "how are you." The door to the bookstore was wide open, and colorful garden books were stacked high on the tables.

Smiling and nodding to friends, we grabbed our blue registration packets, plunked them down on two seats toward the front of the auditorium, and flew back outside to the big lawn where the plant vendors had their

92

booths. Six blue and white striped canopies were set up to shade the merchants and their loot. Hardy Planters were crowded around the tables banging into each other with boxes full of perennials.

"Why don't you start at this corner and I'll start on the opposite end," I said. "We can meet in the middle and report to each other."

"Good idea," Sandy said. "That way we'll cover our bases twice as fast."

If you think gardeners are peaceful people, you haven't seen them at a plant sale. They jostle each other for the best spot at the table, holding plant boxes chest-high like armor to block rivals from the front lines. Small gardeners duck in front of larger ones like VW Beetles darting in front of trucks. My usual technique is to inch close to the table and then slowly but surely slide along like a slug without giving up my position. But now I had trouble getting anywhere. Each time I headed for a vendor to check out the plants, another long-lost friend came up for a joyful reunion.

"I think I'm about finished with shrub roses," Patricia said with a scowl. "I had to get clear underneath one to prune it so I could get my car in the driveway. Those thorns just ripped me to shreds." She showed me her arms, covered with red welts.

"I know, those roses are such bullies," I commiserated, sneaking a glance at a sale table nearby, full of pink and purple clematis. "I'm all torn up too." I held out the backs of my hands, full of scratches. We were veterans of plant wars comparing our battle scars.

As we talked on, I watched the parade of gardeners marching by with boxes full of plants. I couldn't bear it anymore. I sidled towards the plant tables with my friend, leading her along as if we were doing some stately English country dance where you lead your partner along with your eyes, no hands. Scanning the plants at last, I spotted one that looked a lot like a rare hardy begonia. As I tipped my head to read the label, a long freckled arm reached in and snagged the treasure. Speechless and bereft, I watched a woman in a bright red sundress shove the begonia into a box already crammed full of perennials.

Before I could say a word, an acquaintance from Canada hailed me, and once again, the conversation kept me from shopping. Looking into my friend's eyes, as we caught up, I finally got it. All these gardeners were the flowers—they were my reason for returning year after year. I had enough plants, and plenty of books. It was this company of kindred spirits that I'd come to partake of, this community of men and women who love gardens and beauty as much as I do.

I decided to forget about buying plants, and it was a good thing I did. Bossy ushers were summoning us inside for the lectures and slide shows.

"Time for the drawings, hurry up, don't miss out!" they warned us, herding us in like sheep.

The only way to get 300 gardeners to stop shopping was bribery. Big potted plants sat on the stage waiting to be given away as door prizes before the speakers would begin. Latecomers would miss out on winning a golden-leaved catalpa, or a rare salvia with blue flowers. The best enticement, a six foot tall arbor, was saved for the last day, and was won by a woman from Spokane. How she got it home will be a story to be told at next year's conference.

Mothers and daughters, sisters, husbands and wives, and groups of friends filed into the hall and sank into their seats. They'd come from as far away as Chicago, Berkeley and Vancouver, B.C. Young gardeners who didn't know a daylily from a lily, and old gardeners who could tell a *Ligularia* from a *Lamiastrum*, sat side by side in the stuffy auditorium, fanning themselves with the program notes, waiting for the first speaker to begin. The conversation was deafening.

"Number 3443. A lovely pot of Agapanthus, courtesy of Daisy Fields Nursery!" the mistress of ceremonies shouted over the microphone. The crowd quieted down, carefully checking their ticket numbers. Shrieks of victory rang out as a tall woman in a T-shirt, shorts and sandals loped up to the stage to claim her prize. Applause and whistles from the audience cheered her on. Several more plants were given away in this fashion before the first speaker was introduced, the lights were dimmed and at last, the slides of gardens began to appear on the big screen.

One after another, designers from Scotland, Britain and Brooklyn narrated the Latin names of plants in their unique regional accents, as they showed exemplary cottage gardens full of irises, peonies and roses. Rock gardens, water gardens, and old-fashioned grandmothers' gardens filled the screen to the sound of oohs and ahs from the audience. Our white-haired, pink-cheeked Scottish speaker showed us slides of his country garden in a remote village with sheep grazing on the distant hills. In one scene an elderly farmhand was building sensational stone walls that we would dream about that night.

A stylishly-dressed designer from New York took us to the tops of Manhattan penthouses where avid gardeners grow all their trees in boxes and find ways to counter wind and pollution. She showed us courtyard gardens carved out of tiny urban front yards and mini-pergolas piled high with honeysuckle and wisteria. The story we will never forget was about the gazebo that she planted with so many vines that it finally collapsed. "I got over it pretty fast," she boasted. We wondered how long it took for her clients to recover.

When we'd had our fill of exotic experts, we poured

out of the auditorium to visit the local plant mavens. Three hundred strong, we scurried for the restrooms, and dashed to pick up box lunches. We rushed to the parking lot and charged off like race car drivers, each of us hoping to be first at the gardens. Big dust clouds filled the campus as vans, trucks and station wagons zoomed off in all directions.

On the second day of the conference the mistress of ceremonies pleaded with us.

"Yesterday, you were all so eager to get to the gardens that you arrived before the garden owners. Kindly give them half an hour or so to get home while you eat your lunch here on the campus."

Her request may have sounded reasonable, but it was hopelessly unrealistic. When 300 gardeners come together, their collective passion for plants and books and beauty gets stirred up to a boiling frenzy. It would be like asking a swarm of bees on a lavender hedge to settle down.

Gardening is often a solitary task, planning and planting in silence, a sacred sort of quiet that allows the imagination to work. So when gardeners get together, at long last, there is so much to talk about, so much to do.

"I love sharing these trips with you," I told my friend Sandy later that afternoon. "You appreciate the beauty but understand that when I'm photographing, I need to be quiet. And just at the right time, you always bring something to my attention that I hadn't noticed."

"And it's so much fun comparing notes in the car on the way back," she said. "It's great to see these gardens, but sharing them makes it even better. I remember traveling by myself to the East Coast one year and I kept looking around for someone to gab to when I'd see something wonderful."

Even for the most sociable Hardy Planters, there's

the small problem of dueling cameras at these events. One gardener stood with camera poised at the end of a long vista, while a second, like a mirror image, stood at the other end. Like an old Marx Brothers movie, they pantomimed to each other. "You first, I'll go second," and then they took turns firing away.

Sandy and I stayed at the last garden far too long, way past the 5 p.m. closing time, but the two owners simply would not stop talking. They too wanted to share. They filled us in on all the work they'd done for the last five years, from making the crushed rock paths to building a potting shed, to hunting down unusual plants. "This Hardy Plant weekend has been so satisfying, "our hostess said. "It's been worth all the effort. Our friends enjoy this place, but they have no appreciation for the plants, and they don't really understand the work we've put into it. They just come here to hang out and relax. You guys know what it takes to make this happen."

"We sure do," I said with a sigh. "I'm going home right now to redo my whole garden."

Sandy and I were pretty quiet on the way home. We'd covered nine gardens in two days, and our minds were racing with new ideas.

"I think that last garden was a little too perfect," I complained. "Too controlled."

"Yeah, too gorgeous," Sandy agreed. "It was finished. And you know a garden is never supposed to be finished."

"Well they did have that big mess on the side that they're going to dig into next year," I reminded her.

"Right," Sandy said, "and the sidewalk that needs repaving, and the trees that have to be taken down because they're about to fall on the house."

We began to feel a little better. It helped to remember the work ahead.

I dropped Sandy off and pulled into my own driveway, suddenly feeling very weary. I opened the door and plopped down on the couch for a cat nap. My body was tired but my mind was still whirling with visions of plants and people. I could hear fragments of conversation from the lectures and garden visits replaying in my head. It felt good to rest my eyes, but I never did fall asleep. Finally I got up and headed out to the garden to start making it over.

Belonging to a Garden

And the end of all our exploring will be to arrive

where we started and know the place for the first time.

—*T. S. Eliot*

JUST THE OTHER DAY I read about a tour of Italian gardens next summer, and a small flame of travel fever shot through me. I let it pass. I know better than that now. I'm staying home this year. I saw enough gorgeous English gardens last fall, and I came down with a bad case of homesickness for my own garden.

We first stepped off the tour bus into a heavenly garden in the Yorkshire countryside. Even the vegetable garden looked like a still life, with tan onions hung to dry against a gray stone wall. Our hostess, Lady Brookfield, led our small group around the garden, tromping through the damp grass in green Wellington boots. There was something about her long stride and rapid pace that irked me. I slowed way down, stopping to admire a rugosa rose hedge studded with shiny red hips. I sauntered over to the pond, and stood and stared at red and yellow maples reflected in the still water. I closed my eyes and turned my face up to feel the sun's warmth. I lagged way behind the group that marched obediently behind our energetic guide and her equally peppy dog. And I found myself thinking about my own rugosa roses back home, loaded with glossy hips, and the pond that I'd like to dig in the back yard. Images of next year's vegetable garden, edged with basil and parsley, drifted through my mind.

At Great Dixter, where two fellows weeded between rows of leeks, I longed to drop to my knees beside them and stick my fingers in the dirt. But the closest I got to touching soil was when another garden owner let us run our hands through his finished compost. Sheer bliss, and terrible pangs of homesickness for my own compost. Later in the trip, I watched from my Edinburgh hotel window as the cook cut chives from a small patch of herbs in the back garden. I wished I were in his shoes. Back home, my garlic chives would be going to seed right now, and I should be there, deadheading them at this very instant. What was I doing looking out the window of a hotel room in Scotland when I wanted to be in Portland, snipping off seedpods? I felt so useless, a passive spectator who could only watch while others gardened to their hearts' content.

Everywhere we went it was the same. At Sissinghurst's cottage garden three young men raked leaves and swept every speck of soil off the narrow sidewalks. My hands itched to grab the broom and sweep the cobbles clean, to seize the rake and pull its metal tines through wet leaves.

At Pitmedden an elderly gardener slowly dug up neat rectangles of sod, stacked them in a wheelbarrow, and trundled them off to the compost pile. It was all I could do not to snatch the spade out of his hands and cut into that lawn myself. I longed to pirate away his ancient wheelbarrow and push it across the crunchy gravel path.

Beth Chatto's garden had a nursery, where I bought some colchicum bulbs that were flowering in their bins. I told the saleswoman to cut off the flowers and put them in water—there was no point in smashing the beautiful purple flowers in my purse. It would be hours before I'd be back in London anywhere near a vase. If only I were home, I could cut the flowers for my own kitchen. I looked forward to getting home and planting the colchicum bulbs.

Even buying English garden magazines made me

homesick. Each magazine was encased in a thick sheet of transparent plastic enclosing a trowel, or a kneeling pad, or a seed packet. Holding that kneepad and trowel in my hand immediately made me wish I were home, kneeling on my own damp grass, troweling out my own weeds. What was I doing on a tour bus in the Yorkshire countryside, reading garden magazines and traipsing through other people's gardens?

Seed packets not only came with the magazines, they were for sale everywhere we stopped, at garden supply stores, at nurseries, even in grocery stores. My favorite place was an old, dark seed store that smelled like potatoes, crammed with bins of bulbs and onion sets and tall racks stuffed with Mr. Fothergill's seed packets. A lovable gent with white, bushy eyebrows and a matching moustache smiled at me from the envelopes. His shirtsleeves were rolled up to show muscular arms. Smoking a pipe and sporting the kind of brown felt hat that my grandfather wore, Mr. Fothergill was leaning on a picket fence, smiling as he should, because all around him orange nasturtiums and purple lupines bloomed, and plump green beans climbed up homemade teepees.

The store manager helped me choose among a dozen promising varieties of cherry tomatoes and a wealth of poppy selections—Icelandic, Shirley, Oriental, Ladybug. I could have stayed there all that rainy afternoon talking about seeds, but oh no, the bus driver came after me to get moving, and we were off to the next garden.

This year I'm staying home. I'll be planting and snipping, raking and sweeping to my heart's content. I'll plant Mr. Fothergill's seeds in my own garden. Like him, I'll be smiling, because I'll be the one surrounded by peach-colored nasturtiums and purple morning glories climbing teepees made from apple branches. I'll be happy because I'll be home, in my own garden, where I belong.

Wedding Bells

Perfectly Imperfect

*Your assumptions are your windows on the world. Scrub
them off every once in a while, or the light won't come in.*

—*Alan Alda*

ONCE UPON A TIME I believed that if I worked very hard and were persistent enough, I would ultimately have a perfect garden. Here was my innocent plan: Each year I would open one or two new beds in my country garden until eventually it would look like Alan Bloom's Bressingham, a vision of colorful perennial islands adrift in an ocean of verdant lawn. I pictured mixed borders all along the perimeters that would knit together in perfectly harmonious color schemes à la Gertrude Jekyll, with flowers in bloom each day of the year à la Margery Fish. I would take Rosemary Verey's advice and never be dull. I would heed Christopher Lloyd's command and add vertical shapes to the beds. I would follow Beth Chatto's example and triangulate my plants. Surely then, it was just a matter of time and effort—in another year or two my garden would be so perfect that guests would sigh with envy and faint with pleasure.

Nothing, however, went according to plan. It's been fourteen years now and the garden grows more and more imperfect each season. My early dream of carving so many beds out of the lawn and planting them so chock-full of perennials that I wouldn't have to mow or weed has backfired. The more I plant, the more there is to tend—to fertilize, mulch, deadhead, prune, and whack back in the fall. Despite the most intensive planting, weeds still sneak in and root down, right in the middle of

103

a perennial crown if that's the only space left. New weeds even more noxious than original natives have traveled in on the coattails of perennials grown from international seed exchanges.

Nobody warned me that despite the best-laid plans, I would keep changing my taste. Pastels were wonderful until I fell in love with red and orange and magenta. The thrill of flowers was surpassed by fascination with foliage. Perennials were a passion until I got hooked by shrubs. Trees began to intrigue me, and vines . . . even annuals and tropicals and terrifying plants like bamboo that I have never dared to grow, except in containers. Each year new cultivars are introduced that I can't resist, with better shapes, longer bloom periods and more colorful leaves.

To further complicate matters, I began to love writing as much as gardening. How wonderful to have two passions, you might think, yet imagine how terrible it is to be torn between two equally irresistible loves! I'd write in the mornings, taking guilty peeks out the window, and promise to give the garden my full attention in the afternoon. I'd garden first thing in the morning, get a great idea for an article right in the middle of weeding, and vow to write it down the minute I got back in the house.

In the best of times, gardening feeds the writing by inspiring ideas for magazine features and books, and time at the keyboard gives my hardworking muscles a breather. In the worst of times, the garden takes all my energy and little is left for writing, or the writing wins out and the poor garden threatens to revert to wilderness. Morning glory and horsetail creep into the borders and choke out the prize plants. Slugs slither to the top of the lily buds and chomp away, and aphids swarm to the tender rose buds as if a big announcement had been made in the universe that I was too busy writing to protect my flowers.

What to do? When I asked Mirabel Osler, author of *A Gentle Plea for Chaos*, how she writes and gardens, she swore that the garden is very forgiving, that it waits until she's done writing a book. When Anna Pavord, author of *The Tulip*, a book heavy enough to use for weightlifting, was visiting Portland, she said that although she loves to garden, she was thoroughly enjoying her roller-coaster book tour all over the world.

I decided to follow these good examples and stay in the moment. I'd give my attention to whatever was in front of me, and trust that the garden would wait when I was writing, and that the writing would wait when I was gardening. If it meant that neither project would be perfect, so be it. I'd give myself to the process and let that be my focus, instead of chasing the impossibly elusive ideal of perfection.

For it's truly in the making of the garden that my heart is happy, and in the smallest pleasures of the day. Looking up from the bed I'm weeding to see an early evening sky streaked with pink and lavender. Noticing that 'Pallida' witch hazel is glowing yellow in the dead of winter, and that the white sasanqua camellia blooming along the fence is actually edged with pink and has a sweet scent.

It is in the discovery of ideas and feelings that the pleasure of writing rests—in stringing together sentences sparkling with juicy words that convey the joy and angst of all those adventures and misadventures out in the perfectly imperfect garden. For who would I be without that jungle that I strive to tame and order, without that small piece of paradise that feeds my soul and nourishes my spirit at the same time it breaks my back and humbles my pride?

Accentuate the Positive

All things in this world are impermanent.

They have the nature to rise and pass away.

To be in harmony with this truth brings true happiness.

—*Buddhist Chant*

SOMETIMES I IMAGINE how frustrated doctors must be. People expect them to do impossible things like ward off death forever, when in fact all they can do is prescribe cures for a few diseases. When it comes to colds, flu, cancer and autoimmune diseases with esoteric names, they're in the dark. Sometimes I feel like I am, too.

I'm only a gardener, but I still get asked impossible questions—how to annihilate slugs, how to eliminate moles, how to obliterate aphids. Don't people realize that the problem is their attitude?

Let's look at the bigger picture. Everyone has to eat, even slugs. It's dinner time and the garden is a banquet table. Ligularia leaves are delicious and hosta foliage is so tasty. The new shoots of yarrow are yummy and dahlia leaves are oh so succulent. What's a little nibble here, a bite there—who will miss the edge of a leaf? After all, most gardeners only care about their flowers, and besides, a little grazing will help the plants branch out and get stockier.

Why must we worry about slugs so much? They're nice and quiet and hardly ever kill anything. Why not fret more about our beloved pets—dogs that dig huge craters and trample the perennials, cats that scratch out new seedlings and hunt birds? Why pick on slugs? Just because they're slimy? Isn't squirting squiggles of liquid slug bait all around the beds and coming out the next morning to the sight of slug trails and wilted remains at odds with the spirit of gardening? And why are moles so upsetting? Granted they destroy our idea of law and order in the garden by thrusting up little hills here and there. They're just doing what comes naturally, tunneling away to make their runs. Sure they spoil our pristine lawns by dotting them with mini-volcanoes. But is that a good enough reason to commit mole murder? Do metal mole traps sticking out of the dirt, or covered over with plastic buckets, add elegance to the garden? Can't we be content to stomp down the hills and smooth them over with a rake? Why must we be so violent? How does it figure that this place of beauty that we create requires traps and poisons?

Aphids too create great panic. Maybe it's because they travel in such big packs. The sight of a tribe of them covering a rose bud sends most gardeners into a rage and they rush for the pesticide. But what will the ladybugs eat if we kill all the aphids? Not to mention the lace wings, the praying mantis, and the birds. It's a big dinner party out in the garden, and who are we to poison all the food?

I've done my share of spraying and baiting and killing. Once in a fit of frustration I even whacked a mole over the head with a shovel. (I still can't believe I did that!) But after decades of gardening it finally dawned on me that the moles and the slugs and the aphids return every year, in just about the same numbers. Why should I waste money on poisons and traps when I could spend it on plants?

I'm probably not cured of being on pest patrol. No doubt one July day I will become incensed at the sight of a lily bud with an ugly slug bite at its heart. It's likely that when *Ligularia* 'Desdemona' looks like Swiss cheese, I'll slip on some surgical gloves, plop the slugs in a coffee can, and slam on the lid. But I'm pretty sure I'll leave the aphids alone and wait for the ladybugs to eat them for dinner. And now I call the moles my "little tillers" when they spit up the freshly-churned earth—they do such a good job of turning the soil that I'm willing to put up with them. As if I have a choice.

Loving What Is

We have two eyes to see two sides of things, but
there must be a third eye which will see everything
at the same time and yet not see anything.

—D. T. Suzuki

IT WAS A HOT August day and the garden looked faded
and fried. I was just back from a trip to San Diego and
spent flowers were everywhere—brown spurges and
tan astilbes, dusty pink roses and bleached hydrangeas.
Sprays of spent lady's mantle hung limply over the paths
like old dust mops, and the ground showed cracks big
enough to swallow a trowel. The grass was a pitiful buff
color punctuated by dandelions in full bloom. Everything
was a mess!

I set up some sprinklers to revive the thirsty plants
and looked around some more, wondering what new
disaster I would find. A coating of blue feathers strewn
on the lawn under the apple tree testified to some terrible
fight. Windfall apples dotted the ground, with yellow
jackets hovering. I made a mental note to set up traps.

Suddenly, I caught a whiff of summersweet (*Clethra*)
on the air and moved closer to the white flower spikes
that looked like a gigantic bridal bouquet. And there
beneath the summersweet was a lovely color echo that I
must have planned last spring. 'Frosty Morn' sedum, with
variegated leaves of a most pleasing cool green hue, was
just showing its little white buds. They reminded me of
a beaded purse.

I stopped to pick a leaf and feel the smooth rubbery
texture, to admire the color close up—pale green
washed with a greenish-white marbling and edged with

creamy white, so refreshing and serene. Nearby a drift of 'Sissinghurst White' lungwort (*Pulmonaria*) was also looking very tranquil, the dark green leaves splashed with white polka dots. As if to join the party, a tall zebra grass added its creamy striped leaves to the arrangement. Maybe the garden wasn't so bad after all.

I stopped to deadhead some 'Blackbird' penstemon. Once the spent brown flowers were gone, the remaining spikes of fresh purple flowers shone. Peeking out from behind the penstemon was an unnamed Lobelia seedling in exactly the same color. I'd picked it up at a perennial conference in North Carolina last August, hoping it would be a rich and vibrant color. What luck! Nearby a select form of pincushion plant (*Knautia macedonica*) that a friend gave me was chiming in with a deep burgundy note. This little trio was enhanced by the mahogany leaves of 'Chocolate' snakeroot (*Eupatorium rugosum* 'Chocolate'), now in its second year and beginning to look substantial.

Only last month, bear's breech (*Acanthus mollis*) had displayed dozens of upright stems filled with mysteriously hooded mauve flowers. Now it had collapsed in the heat, stems leaning this way and that, like so many exhausted snakes. I'll cut them back later, I thought, as I set up a sprinkler to revive the parched hydrangeas.

'David' fuchsia was happily blooming its head off, hundreds of tiny red and purple pagoda flowers dangling from the branches. Nearby 'Scarlet Mediland' rose had blossoms of just the same luscious lipstick red. A variegated sedge (*Carex morrowii* 'Aureovariegata') and 'Alexander' loosestrife (*Lysimachia punctata* 'Alexander') offered creamy leaves to accompany the red flowers of the fuchsia and rose.

In the midst of late summer's decline, there was still plenty of beauty—maybe not the freshness of spring or the exuberance of early summer, but still, all was not lost. Soon the heat would diminish and autumn's occasional early rains would quench the garden's thirst. The last late surge of rose bloom would renew the borders, and asters would add clouds of purple and white. August would wane and September would arrive . . . nothing is forever.

The garden comes and goes, dying and blooming, ebbing and flowing, constantly in flux. If we can just accept that, tending the garden becomes a much more fluid process in which we collaborate, rather than one we desperately struggle to control.

Patience

Gardens are not created or made, they unfold,

spiraling open like the silk petals of an evening primrose

flower to reveal the ground plot of the mind and heart

of the gardener and the good earth.

—Wendy Johnson

"THIS YEAR I'M gonna train you up this fence and you're not gonna like it, but you're gonna do it anyhow, and you'll look beautiful!"

These are a gardener's firm words to her clematis in the winter. You have to build up to these things, preparing yourself and your plants for the journey ahead. Talking to plants is a lot like talking to yourself in the car—it's a good way to mull things over in order to get clear. Plants are great listeners. They never interrupt, change the subject or disagree. They might give a little rustle once in a while, but that's it.

If they hear me talking to them, they pay me no mind. "Up, up, up!" I holler at a grape vine as I throw it over the metal grid that forms the ceiling of the arbor. It stays up for a minute and then slyly slides back down. I get the twine. Sometimes it takes more than words.

I tie these woody canes to the wire with firm double knots. There's plenty of leeway for them to sway, but they can only go so far. Plants may not have legs but they've learned to travel, flinging branches here and there and creeping underground by roots and rhizomes.

Vines may not shout "No!" out loud, but they certainly act very contrary. All my roses climb over to the neighbor's side of the fence—I have to sneak over there at night to send them home. My clematis tangles around itself in a big knot instead of traveling up the trellis in a calm, orderly fashion. I spend hours unraveling tendrils and weaving them carefully through the lattice. If I rush or yank too hard, I pay the price of broken stems and ruined flowers.

Whether I like it or not, the plants slow me down. I must pay careful attention, training them, pruning them, mulching them, and fertilizing them, or they won't bloom well, and they'll end up twisted around themselves. We are in this together, the plants and I. The better I tend them, the more they flourish.

Can I be this patient with myself? When the shoot of an idea sprouts, can I quietly watch and see how it unfolds? Can I slow down enough to undo the knots of my sadness, the same way I slow down to untwist a vine? Can I snip away destructive thoughts before I make myself unhappy? Can I feed myself enough quiet and solitude to bloom? Can I spend time with a friend just carefully listening as their thoughts and feelings blossom? Attention is the greatest gift to give, the most satisfying gift to receive.

The plants are great teachers, and their lessons are way beyond horticulture. By connecting with the garden, I learn about relating to myself, and to the people I love. After all, the garden is teeming with all forms of life—plants, bugs, birds, frogs, moles—all growing in their own particular way. It's only natural, then, that as gardeners, we stop every now and then to reflect on our own unfolding.

Acceptance

The mystery of life is not a problem to be solved

but a reality to be experienced.

—Aart Van Der Leeuw

FOR THE SIXTEENTH year, I am weeding my garden this warm August morning, troweling out of the ground morning glory, oxalis, milkweed, dandelions and many more weeds whose names I've made up. There's the green and red weed that spreads itself flat on the ground in late summer, the tall-weed-with-tiny-leaves-and-pink-flowers-at-the-tips that hides amid similar leaves until the pink gives it away. Then there are the plants that have become weeds to me because they grow unreasonably, spreading by root, runner and seed. Some of these even have endearing names like lady's mantle, love-in-a-mist, and forget-me-not, while others caution you with their names, if only you took their names seriously to begin with—bugleweed, goutweed, loosestrife, 'Chameleon' spurge. . . .

But weeding this year is different than in years past. I'm no longer a mad warrior protecting my plants, but more like a mother braiding her daughter's hair, carefully combing out the snaggles with patience and love.

The impossibility of getting rid of weeds has finally sunk in to that deepest level of understanding where acceptance roots down. Most years I've lived under the illusion that if I planted tightly enough, mulched heavily, and kept on top of the weeding early in the season, the garden would eventually have fewer and fewer weeds, until one day the weeds would be gone.

This kind of thinking goes along with the same hope

that some day I would be without weeds in my life—I would rise above anger, never get crabby, quit feeling discouraged. In short, I would become perfectly even-tempered, kind and compassionate, and live out my life as a wise, contemplative, creative woman. But the truth is that just as weeds continue to grow, moods come and go, weather blows hot and cold, cars and washing machines work, then break, and cherished friends move out of town. Every time I pull a weed another one is seeding down somewhere else in the garden. To garden is to weed. To live is to move through the moods, the weather, the changes, with as much grace as we can, understanding that this is the way it is.

Some day perhaps an inventor will come up with the perfect weed prevention device—a spray, a soil amendment, some technique that takes weeds out of the loop. But I hope not. Weeding is perfect practice for tending our plants and our lives . . . doing the best we can to clean up our gardens and clean up our acts, yet understanding that it's an ongoing process that has no end point. Learning with time and practice to do it with grace, with ease, with a smile, without making an enemy of the weeds, or of our own mistakes.

Birds of a Feather

It wasn't that I didn't care what my friend was saying;

it's just that the garden, especially in the summer, comes

in and out of the mind like a love affair.

—*Ann Raver*

BEFORE I MOVED to my second garden, I lived in what I thought of as "my old life," with plenty of time to see friends, go to lunch and do ordinary weekend things like shop for clothes and go to the movies. Suddenly, all those activities seemed very unimportant. It was March and hundreds of perennials from my old garden were waiting in line to be planted. Peonies and irises were falling over the sides of flats. Daffodils stuffed into buckets of sawdust bloomed before I had a chance to plant them. Blueberry shrubs and a dogwood tree bulged out of whiskey barrels.

So what was I to do when my friend Julie, a social worker from my "old life," dropped by expecting to visit, just like we always had done? I fixed us breakfast—scrambled eggs and sourdough toast with homemade blackberry jam and freshly brewed coffee. But as we sat at the dining room table talking and eating, I kept sneaking peeks out the window, trying to imagine the mixed border I wanted to plant to screen out the road. I realized with a guilty twinge that I wished Julie would leave. I was dying to get my hands in the dirt.

"You're so driven!" Julie complained, as if she could read my mind. "You're a million miles away, probably thinking about that damn garden!"

"No, no, just a little spaced out from all the work I've been doing lately," I fibbed. "I'm sorry, I guess I'm preoccupied and not very good company today."

"It's just not much fun coming here anymore," she said, frowning. "I wish you would take a break from all this."

"I'm sure I will after a while," I apologized. "This is like a new job, or having a baby. At first, it's consuming, but in a month or two, I'm sure I'll settle in and relax."

Who was I kidding? I'm not the kind of woman who relaxes. Obsessing is what I do best. If you want to put it in a kinder light, you could say that I'm very focused. When I decided to learn about perennials, that's all I did for two years. I took classes, joined plant societies, went to see gardens. I'm goal-oriented and focused, but driven? Julie was going too far. She just didn't understand me.

La Verne, on the other hand, did. A health care administrator who wore suits and high heels, she came to visit carrying a shopping bag of work clothes and waterproof boots. She clattered into the house only long enough to change, and came back out to weed with me, dressed like a farmer. We plopped down on opposite sides of a border that was only six feet wide, the better to talk across as our fingers reached around the Michaelmas daisies, yanking out grasses and cresses. The weeds flew as fast as the words. To this day I call that bed "The La Verne Bed."

Not that La Verne was any more of a gardener than Julie was. "Which ones are the weeds, Barbara? These ferny little things that look like carrot tops?" she asked, pointing to Queen Anne's lace.

"Yeah, those and the long stringy ones with the little white flowers on the end," I said, pointing to the ground morning glory.

"Dandelions, I can spot those," La Verne assured me, "but I'm not sure about the rest. What are these little gray things?"

"Moss campion—you can leave those in the ground. They'll get electric pink flowers in June," I explained. La Verne wasn't a gardener, but she saw right into my heart and knew I was bitten by the garden. A friend of the heart, she joined me and spent time with me where I needed to be. We could have been knitting or crocheting together, stringing beans or shelling peas. The main thing is that we were together, working and talking as women have for centuries.

Every so often someone comes along who really understands how I live my life. One summer day my friend, Ellen, a sculptor, brought her friend Maria to see the garden. Maria was a painter, and she wanted to photograph the garden and use the slides for inspiration.

Ellen and I strolled around the garden, stopping to admire the roses and asters. Maria set up her tripod and began shooting. By early evening, around seven, the light was perfect, soft and gentle, making the flowers glow.

"I don't want to keep you from dinner or any evening plans," Maria said, but it was plain to me that she was just being polite. I could tell from the way she was still studying the garden that she wanted to linger and photograph some more.

"Don't be silly," I replied. "As long as it's light out, this is where I want to be. Don't tell me you stop painting when the clock says it's dinnertime."

Maria laughed. "No way. You know what it's like. When you get started on a painting, you're in another world. Time stops. You forget what day it is—most of the time I have no idea if it's a weekday or a weekend."

"I know," I agreed. "Most of my friends have two lives—work days, and the rest of the time, evenings and weekends and vacations. My life is all one piece, work and friends all woven together. My hobby became my work, so my work and my play are the same."

"That's right," Ellen said. "It's a way of life."

"You put your finger on it, Ellen," I said. "I try to explain to friends that I'm not earning a living at this—I do this to keep living. You really understand."

After Ellen and Maria left, I felt at peace. These women were a lot like me, connected to their work in a way that was different from having a job. I didn't have to explain myself to them—they were just as involved as I was. From then on, I stopped apologizing for my way of life.

I began to understand myself better after that conversation. The garden keeps me wondering, keeps me dreaming, feeds me with its beauty. It challenges me, frustrates me, nourishes me. It also supports me financially. Yes, I do this for a living. But most of all, I do this for a life.